LIBRARY MANUALS

Volume 6

A HANDBOOK OF CLASSIFICATION AND CATALOGUING

A HANDBOOK OF CLASSIFICATION AND CATALOGUING
For School and College Librarians

MARGARET S. TAYLOR

LONDON AND NEW YORK

First published in 1939 by George Allen & Unwin Ltd

This edition first published in 2022
by Routledge
4 Park Square, Milton Park, Abingdon, Oxon OX14 4RN

and by Routledge
605 Third Avenue, New York, NY 10017

Routledge is an imprint of the Taylor & Francis Group, an informa business

Copyright © 1939 by Taylor & Francis.

All rights reserved. No part of this book may be reprinted or reproduced or utilised in any form or by any electronic, mechanical, or other means, now known or hereafter invented, including photocopying and recording, or in any information storage or retrieval system, without permission in writing from the publishers.

Trademark notice: Product or corporate names may be trademarks or registered trademarks, and are used only for identification and explanation without intent to infringe.

British Library Cataloguing in Publication Data
A catalogue record for this book is available from the British Library

ISBN: 978-1-03-213109-2 (Set)
ISBN: 978-1-00-322771-7 (Set) (ebk)
ISBN: 978-1-03-213296-9 (Volume 6) (hbk)
ISBN: 978-1-03-213300-3 (Volume 6) (pbk)
ISBN: 978-1-00-322855-4 (Volume 6) (ebk)

DOI: 10.4324/9781003228554

Publisher's Note
The publisher has gone to great lengths to ensure the quality of this reprint but points out that some imperfections in the original copies may be apparent.

Disclaimer
The publisher has made every effort to trace copyright holders and would welcome correspondence from those they have been unable to trace.

A HANDBOOK OF CLASSIFICATION AND CATALOGUING
FOR SCHOOL AND COLLEGE LIBRARIANS

by

MARGARET S. TAYLOR

M.A., F.L.A.

Lecturer in Classification and Cataloguing at the London University School of Librarianship

LONDON
GEORGE ALLEN & UNWIN LTD
MUSEUM STREET

FIRST PUBLISHED IN 1939

ALL RIGHTS RESERVED

PRINTED IN GREAT BRITAIN
in 11-Point Plantin Type
BY UNWIN BROTHERS LIMITED
WOKING

GENERAL INTRODUCTION TO THE SERIES

by W. E. DOUBLEDAY, HON. F.L.A.

THIS new Series of Handbooks is intended to supplement the larger Manuals issued by Messrs. George Allen & Unwin and the Library Association under the title of *The Library Association Series of Library Manuals*.

There are some aspects of Library Work which, although by no means unimportant, are of themselves insufficient to require a full-sized manual, and there are other phases which in a comprehensive textbook of manageable dimensions could be dealt with only in a general way. The Handbooks will adequately cover these subjects and will also treat of certain special topics which hitherto have escaped the attention which they deserve, or which—owing to recent developments —demand reconsideration.

Since Library practice must always be in accordance with the particular requirements of different types and sizes of Libraries, variant methods will be indicated from time to time, and a working basis for individual adoption and comparative study will thus be provided. University, Municipal, School, and Special Libraries —rural as well as urban—will be comprehended within the scope of the Practical Library Handbooks, and in each instance the latest advances will be described.

8 CLASSIFICATION AND CATALOGUING

This smaller Series is issued independently by Messrs. George Allen & Unwin Ltd., and the range is sufficiently wide to make the volumes appeal to Administrators, Librarians, Assistants, and Students who intend to sit at the professional examinations. It is hoped that they will be of great practical assistance for immediate use in enhancing and forwarding still further that improvement in Library service which has been so marked since the passing of the Public Libraries Act of 1919.

CONTENTS

CHAPTER		PAGE
I.	THE NATURE OF BOOK CLASSIFICATION	11
II.	SCHEMES SUITABLE FOR SCHOOL LIBRARIES	20
III.	HOW TO APPLY A CLASSIFICATION SCHEME	37
IV.	KINDS OF CATALOGUES. DISPLAY. MAKE-UP OF ENTRY	49
V.	THE AUTHOR AND TITLE CATALOGUE—AUTHOR ENTRIES	59
VI.	THE AUTHOR AND TITLE CATALOGUE—TITLE ENTRIES	79
VII.	SUBJECT AND FORM CATALOGUES	90
VIII.	SUBJECT AND FORM CATALOGUES (*continued*)	103
	INDEX	119

CHAPTER ONE

THE NATURE OF BOOK CLASSIFICATION

THE first duty of the librarian is to ensure that books in the library can be readily found. One reader will require a single book by an author, another several works by one author, while a third seeks information on a particular subject. All such inquiries can certainly be met by author and subject catalogues, but much time will be wasted in meeting subject demands unless the library is arranged according to a classification scheme.

A book classification divides the whole of Knowledge into a number of broad groups, e.g. History, Science, Religion, etc. These are subdivided further and further until quite specific subjects are reached and it is no longer practical to continue the process. For example, one of the divisions of Science is Zoology. This division can again be split up into groups of animals, e.g. Fishes, Birds, etc. A large university library, which caters for specialist scholars and research workers, would need more minute subdivision, but "Fishes" is sufficiently specific for the average-sized school library.

As the repetition of the name of Main Class, Division, and Subdivision (e.g. Science—Zoology—Fishes) would be very wearisome and make location of books difficult, a notation is used to represent subjects and show where they appear in the scheme. Either letters, or figures, or both may be used. The important thing about notation is that it should show sequence. For example, in the Dewey Decimal scheme, all Science books bear the number 500, Zoology 590 (i.e. the ninth division of Science), and those on Fishes 597 (i.e. the seventh subdivision of the ninth division of the fifth main class). Books are arranged on the shelves in this numerical sequence—or alphabetical sequence if the notation consists of letters.

A classification mark, or number, is a symbol for a particular subject and all books on that subject must be classified in the same place. Thus, if the Dewey Decimal scheme is chosen, all books on Fishes will be numbered 597. This is an elementary point, but often causes confusion to the beginner. If the librarian wishes to individualize every book, he can put the first three letters of the author's name after the class mark.

The class mark is quite independent of the shelves. Certainly, the 597 books will follow the 596, and all the 590 will follow the 580. In the same way, if a letter notation is used, the A group will precede the B, and the AA division come before the AB. But a book is not fixed to a particular shelf; groups of books are not confined to one case. Hence, if there is an unexpected growth in a certain section and all the allotted shelves full, other sections can be moved on leaving room for additions without the necessity for altering hundreds of class marks.

THE NATURE OF BOOK CLASSIFICATION 13

With the old method of "fixed location" the stock was divided into broad subject groups, e.g. Science, History, etc., and perhaps these split up once again into divisions, e.g. Physics, Chemistry, Botany, Zoology, etc. A set of cases was put aside for each group, so many shelves per division, and each book numbered according to its case, shelf, and position on that shelf. Initial letters were generally used to denote the main groups. Thus, if History were represented by H and the first set of shelves devoted to General and Ancient history, Stobart's "The Grandeur that was Rome" would bear the location mark, H.I.5.g. because it was the seventh book on the fifth shelf of the first tier or case. Trouble arose when the Ancient history section became full. New books could not be inserted without moving on all the English and European history books and spending a vast amount of time in altering shelf marks. This shows the impossibility of working "fixed location" in a growing, expanding library. Classification does not tie a book down to a certain position on a particular shelf, so does not interfere with future development.

This mobility is not a disadvantage if pupils are taught to use the library intelligently and find what they want by means of subject marks. Your classification tables will be equipped with an alphabetical index. If Dewey is used, a boy will find the number 597 against Fishes. He should have been taught enough about the arrangement of the library to understand that all books on Fishes will be numbered 597 and be able to find them by locating this number. He will not be upset if, next time, they have been moved a shelf lower, since he works by subject or class marks, not shelf position. This method will stand him in good stead when he uses other libraries after leaving school.

Besides the advantage of a flexible arrangement, whereby new books can be inserted in their most useful places without upsetting the whole library, it is very convenient to have large, unwieldy groups of subjects broken up so that books on a specific subject come together. Take History, for example. Not only are English history books separated from general European, but these are subdivided according to period and district. In the Art class, Architecture books come together, Sculpture, Painting, and so on. This helps both reader and librarian when hunting for information, and it is also of great value to the librarian in showing the relative strength and weakness of the different sections. It is far easier to keep the stock of a classified library well-balanced, without some subjects being overlooked.

A classified library has a certain educational value. Pupils get a bird's-eye view of the whole realm of knowledge and learn to appreciate the intersection of its different branches. Their own studies take on a new significance when they see the relation of these to other subjects, while the browsing boy or girl is stimulated to explore further fields.

When selecting a classification, school librarians have

a choice of several bibliographical schemes. These will be examined in detail in the next chapter. First, comes the Dewey Decimal, which is widely used in municipal, county, university, and special libraries, and is equally suitable for school libraries. The Cheltenham classification was only published fully in 1937, but has been used at Cheltenham Ladies' College for nearly thirty years. It was drawn up specially for a school library. The Bliss classification is a general bibliographical scheme and has attracted a good deal of attention from school librarians because of the logical arrangement of subjects.

There are two other important modern schemes, but these do not suit school libraries. The Library of Congress classification is excellent in many ways and will be found in several university libraries, where extremely detailed subdivision is needed. Such detail would be a burden in a school library. The scheme cannot be abridged like the Dewey Decimal. Another disadvantage is that the tables occupy more than twenty volumes and, unless the classifier knows the scheme very well, the process of classifying is considerably slowed up. There is no cumulative index yet. Brown's Subject scheme will be found in many public libraries, but the arrangement of some subjects is most unusual and would prove confusing in a school library.

The alternative to adopting one of these bibliographical classifications is to make a scheme of one's own. Librarians are strongly warned against taking this course. Not only should the maker of a classification be an expert in every subject, or be able to obtain advice from experts, but he needs an unusually well-balanced, impartial attitude to the whole of knowledge. In addition, he should have had considerable experience in the use of classification schemes and in their application to books. The history specialist may work out the history divisions admirably, but be inclined to lose interest when he comes to other subjects. The librarian may obtain the help of other members of the staff, each working out the details of his own subject, but results will not be satisfactory unless the librarian can coordinate these divisions into a well-balanced whole. This is far more difficult than the new enthusiast can realize. Moreover, there are so many practical "snags" which often do not show until the scheme has been working for a time. The only way to rectify them is to alter that part of the scheme and undertake the lengthy task of reclassifying a hundred or more books.

I am aware that some "home-made" classifications have proved satisfactory, but only a few. The majority of school librarians who have attempted to make them regret the experiment very soon and are only too anxious to change over to Dewey or Cheltenham or Bliss. These schemes passed through an experimental stage, lasting from two to thirty years, before appearing in print for general use. During that time, they were tried out in libraries and altered as practical considerations demanded. Bliss took ten years to outline his

THE NATURE OF BOOK CLASSIFICATION 17

classification, apply it to a library, and readjust it. From 1912 until its first publication in 1935, he explains that it was further expanded and altered. Few, if any, school librarians can spare the time that classification-making requires. They have their other library duties of book selecting, ordering, accessioning, cataloguing, and routine administration, so that it seems foolish to undertake a lengthy, arduous task which is really quite unnecessary.

Three published schemes have been mentioned as suited to the needs of school libraries. Their respective merits and demerits are hotly debated, so librarians are advised to make a study of all three before coming to a decision. It will be found useful to compare them according to the following points.

Consider the arrangement of subjects. Do you think it important that classes should follow one another in logical order? If so, choose a scheme which has a philosophical basis. Does any scheme separate subjects that are cognate? Is subdivision too detailed, or not sufficiently worked out? Broad divisions, which mean that there will be a hundred or more books bearing the same class number, are not practical. On the other hand, the school library does not require the extreme detail of the Library of Congress classification where there are numbers for individual species of insects and for different editions of the more famous classics.

Notations should be carefully compared. When letters of the alphabet are used there may be twenty-six main classes, but arabic numerals can only give ten. This does not provide such a broad base. At the next stage of division, two numerals only yield a hundred places, but two letters will provide for twenty-six times twenty-six subjects. Thus, a letter notation means that class marks are shorter than if numerals are used. Shorter marks are usually easier to grasp, but many school librarians say this advantage is lost because the modern child no longer learns the alphabet by heart and does not know the order of letters.

Finally, the general make-up of a classification should be considered. The tables should be printed in clear type, with main classes, divisions, etc., clearly indicated. There should be an alphabetical index of subjects with their respective class marks, so that the classifier can quickly locate any subject in the tables.

It is a good plan to have at least one copy of the scheme rebound in a heavy binding, which will stand constant wear, and interleaved with blank pages. The school librarian can then note alterations, special decisions, etc., opposite the appropriate place in the printed tables.

A few minor alterations to any published scheme seem inevitable to suit individual needs. These should be clearly shown in the tables and recorded in the index. Unless this is done there is great danger of confusion later on, when an alteration may be forgotten or the classifying is done by someone else.

Whenever possible alterations should be avoided and

they certainly must be kept down to a minimum. Modifications are often regretted in a few months and the original arrangement then seen to have been far more practical. School librarians should consider carefully before introducing any, and only do so when convinced of the necessity. Then they should be regarded as temporary until thoroughly tested by use.

CHAPTER TWO

SCHEMES SUITABLE FOR SCHOOL LIBRARIES

I. THE DEWEY DECIMAL CLASSIFICATION

THE Dewey Decimal Classification is unquestionably the most popular scheme in Great Britain, the Dominions, the Colonies, and the United States. It has been translated into the principal European languages and also into Chinese and Japanese. It can be used with equal success in small and large libraries, while for highly specialized collections and for detailed bibliographical work, there is an expanded form known as the Classification Décimale Universelle.

The scheme is American in origin. It was first published in 1876 and was the work of a certain Melvil Dewey, sub-librarian of Amherst College, Massachussetts. Dewey died in 1931, but for many years before his death experts had helped in revising and expanding the scheme. The original work was comparatively slight, as may be seen by comparing the 1876 edition with the 1932 (the thirteenth) edition. In the first publication, the actual tables of classification only occupied twelve pages. By 1932, these had grown to nine hundred and two. Copyrights and control of all editions now belong to the Lake Placid Club Education Foundation. Melvil

Dewey made this arrangement in 1922, but stipulated that money received from future editions must only be spent on improving the scheme, once the cost of production and other necessary expenses had been met, "thereby preventing possibility that the work should ever be made a source of either personal or institutional profit."

Besides the full scheme, there is an abridged version in which the classification tables are reduced from nine hundred and two pages to fifty-six. School libraries will find this carries subdivision far enough. The full scheme goes into details that are only required by libraries with very large book stocks, and, though it is possible to cut the tables down onself—e.g. only to classify to one decimal place—the index is then rendered useless. It is more satisfactory to use the abridged version. This is called, "Abridged decimal classification and relative index, by Melvil Dewey, A.M., LL.D., for libraries and personal use in arranging for immediate reference books, pamphlets, clippings, pictures, manuscript notes and other material."[1] The fifth edition was published in 1936 (and reprinted in 1938) by the Lake Placid Club, New York. Copies can be ordered through any English bookseller and the cost, at the present rate of exchange, is twelve shillings and sixpence.

All knowledge is divided into ten classes. Philosophy

[1] All Dewey numbers quoted in this book are taken from the 1936 abridged edition.

is Class 100, Religion 200, Sociology 300, Philology 400, Science 500, Useful arts 600, Fine arts 700, Literature 800, History, Biography and Travel 900. Very general works covering a large number of subjects (e.g. the "Encyclopaedia Britannica") come in the 000, General Works class. Each class is subdivided into nine divisions. For example, Science splits into 510 Mathematics, 520 Astronomy, 530 Physics, 540 Chemistry, 550 Geology and Physical geography, 560 Palaeontology, 570 Biology and Anthropology, 580 Botany, 590 Zoology. Works concerned with Science in general remain at 500. Once again, these subdivisions are broken up, e.g. 591 Physiological zoology, 592 Invertebrates, and so on. At the fourth stage, a decimal point is added and then division can proceed indefinitely—as required.

e.g. 500 Science   800 Literature
     590 Zoology   820 English literature
       598 Birds and reptiles   822 English drama
         598·1 Reptiles   822·3 Shakespeare

In the abridged version, subdivision seldom goes beyond one decimal place. There is a very full alphabetical index which guides the classifier to the place of any subject in the tables.

e.g. Habakkuk   Bible   224
     Habeas corpus   law   347
     Habit   psychology   158
     Habitations, animal zoology   591·5
     Habitations, human hygiene   613

General reference books go in the 000 class. The Philosophy (100) class includes Psychology and Ethics. Religion (200) splits into four main groups. General religious topics (Christian and Nonchristian) go from 200 to 219, the Bible and its parts from 220 to 229, Christian theology and Church bodies from 230 to 289, and Nonchristian (including Mythology) from 290 to 299.

Sociology (300) is a rather confusing class. Its main divisions are Statistics (310), Political science (320), Economics (330), Law (340), Administration (350), Welfare and social societies (360), Education (370), Commerce (380), and Customs (390). This class should have been placed next to History, which is right at the end of the scheme, 900 to 999. History is arranged according to countries, grouped under the continents for modern history, from 940 to 999. For example, History of Asia is 950, China 951, Japan 952, Arabia 953, India 954, etc. Ancient history is 930 to 939, and separated from General history (900 to 909) by Topography and Biography. Recognized modifications are the placings of travel books in history with a distinguishing T (e.g. History of England is 942, so Travel in England would be 942 T), and the scattering of lives among the subjects for which the biographees were famous. Thus, a life of Oliver Cromwell would be placed in the Stuart period subdivision of English History, 942·06.

Another annoying separation is the gulf between

24 CLASSIFICATION AND CATALOGUING

Philology (400) and Literature (800). The first factor of division in both classes is language. The same numbers are used for linguistic subdivision, except that 410 is Comparative philology and 810 American literature. Apart from this, the divisions are alike, e.g. 420 English philology, 820 English literature; 430 German philology, 830 German literature; 440 French philology, 840 French literature, etc. In the 400 class, each language is subdivided into Orthography, Etymology, Dictionaries, Synonyms, Grammars, Prosody, Dialects, and Texts for learning the language. The literatures are divided according to forms, e.g. Poetry, Drama, etc.

The remaining classes cover Pure science (500), Useful arts (600), and Fine arts (700). Recreations and games go in 700.

The notation of the Dewey Decimal scheme is very easily grasped and many class marks are unconsciously memorized by users, e.g. 942 English history. This is an advantage in locating books quickly; also, when classifying new ones. It is claimed that arabic numerals are much easier to remember than letters, that they are quicker to write, and that there is less danger of mistakes being made in copying them. Undoubtedly, Dewey's system of class marks is extremely simple and, by the introduction of a decimal point, subdivision can be carried as far as required. The provision for indefinite subdivision is essential to a classification because entirely new subjects will arise and have to be fitted into their correct places, e.g. Television, Air raid precautions. The simple, flexible and easily memorized notation has been one of the reasons for the wide popularity of this scheme.

The chief objections raised against the Dewey Decimal classification are its separation of many cognate subjects, the lack of any philosophical or logical order in its classes, etc., its American bias, and—a somewhat minor point—the use of simplified spelling in the tables. The separation of Sociology from History and again, Philology from Literature, is to be condemned. A remedy is to break the numerical order and to put the 300 class next to the 900, 400 next to 800. Then there are no satisfactory places for history books on the Mediterranean, Pacific, and so on. Often the arrangement of subjects, general and specific, is quite arbitrary and seems strained to fit the notation, and no one can claim that one main class merges into the next in a logical, progressive order, as in the Bliss scheme. Whether this matters or not is another question. The opinion is often expressed that book classification exists for the *convenient* arrangement of library stocks and, therefore, should not be confused with Philosophical classification or Methodology. Thirdly, there is the American bias. For example, American literature precedes English, although, historically, it developed later and should follow English. This does not affect the bulk of the scheme. The simplified spelling is again irritating, but will only be apparent to users of the actual tables—that is, those classifying books.

But, whatever the faults of the Dewey Decimal classification, one cannot get away from the fact that it is extraordinarily popular in libraries of all kinds and sizes. It does fulfil the need for a convenient method of arranging books. This wide use of the scheme is a strong argument for its adoption in school libraries, since scholars will then become familiar with a method of arrangement they are likely to encounter in other libraries. Secondly, it has this ideally simple notation, which makes it very easy to apply and to work. It is published in an abridged form, with just the amount of subdivision that a school library requires. Finally, it is a "live" scheme, that is, kept up-to-date by experts. Revised editions, incorporating new discoveries and additions to knowledge, are published at regular intervals.

II. THE CHELTENHAM CLASSIFICATION

The Cheltenham classification was applied to the library of the Cheltenham Ladies' College nearly thirty years ago, but did not appear fully in print until 1937. The original scheme was altered and expanded during its pre-publication period. The authors acknowledge inspiration from a bibliographical classification of the late nineteenth century, called "Perkins' Rational," but, although a few features of that scheme have been incorporated, the Cheltenham classification is essentially an original piece of work, compiled for a single type of library—that belonging to a school. The authors explain that it "is offered for the use of those who prefer that the arrangement of the Library should be on similar lines to those on which subjects are taught."

One complaint against general bibliographical schemes by school libraries is that, owing to the influence of the school curriculum on stock, the main classes are extremely disproportionate. In a Dewey-classified library, the Literature class will be several times larger than most of the others. There are gaps in divisions of a class like Philosophy which will probably never be filled. Such disadvantages do not occur in the Cheltenham scheme, since it has a very well-balanced arrangement of subjects, according to the school library's requirements. Philology and Literature are put together under each language and occupy seven main classes, instead of two, as in Dewey. There is a main class for Geography, an important school subject. Geology is included here, rather than under Science, because it is usually taught by the Geography master or mistress. There is a special class for Junior books and one for Fiction. The main class of History follows its cousin, Sociology.

Divisions and subdivisions are worked out simply, but in sufficient detail. Further expansion is permissible, if required. "As this scheme is for use in a School Library, we have not subdivided minutely in cases where one would not expect to find many books on a subject. Thus, we have given a place for Oriental Religions, A 32, and if the Library possesses only some half-dozen books on all these religions, A 32 will be enough for finding—or other—purposes. If, however,

28 CLASSIFICATION AND CATALOGUING

the Library has enough books on this subject to make it worth while to subdivide further, then a figure after a decimal point may be given for each subdivision. If this is done, the subdivisions should be added in the tables and the extra figure added to the entries in the index, where only the main figure A 32 is given for Buddhism, Confucianism, Mohammedanism."

A useful feature of the scheme is the provision of alternatives. For example, Greek and Roman sculpture books may be placed in Class S (Fine arts) or, if preferred in K, where there is a division for Greek and Roman archaeology and antiquities under Classical language and literature. Church history can be put in A (Theology) or D (History). Food and food values can be either Domestic economy or Chemical technology; the authors add, "Boys' and Girls' schools will probably differ here." There are other cases of these alternatives, which are undoubtedly of much practical value and do away with the need for individual modifications.

The notation consists of letters and arabic numerals. Each main class is denoted by a letter, e.g. F stands for French language and literature, K for Classics, M for Science. In only a few cases has the initial capital letter of a subject been used for the notation. This is not a good practice since it is apt to be misleading. A boy notices that F stands for French language and literature, G for German, and is then apt to expect that H should be History, S Science, whereas to arrange subjects by their alphabetical position would not be classification. The partial practice is confusing, too. Why should G be

SCHEMES FOR SCHOOL LIBRARIES

German rather than Geography, or Gardening, or Geometry, or Great Britain? These "literal mnemonics" are better avoided altogether, but the Cheltenham scheme only offends in three instances. Bliss introduces at least fifty.

Division continues by means of arabic numerals from 1 to 100. Further subdivision can be made by using decimals.

e.g. D HISTORY
    21 Modern European history: general
      ·1 A.D. 476–1453: general
        ·11 476–1100 (including Normans)
        ·12 1100–1453 (including Crusades)
        ·13 Holy Roman Empire
      ·2 1453–1815: general
        ·21 1453–1610
        ·22 1610–1715

Roman numerals have been used in the printed tables to indicate the main divisions of a class, but are ignored when classifying; the arabic numbers run consecutively through a class.

e.g. C SOCIOLOGY
    I GENERAL
      1 General treatises
        ·1 History
        ·2 Biography
      2 Social organization and conditions
      3 Statistics
    II LAW
      4 General treatises. Constitutional law
      5 International law
        etc.

These roman numerals, or "chapter headings," were used in the Perkins' scheme, but it is a pity they have been included. As they do not affect the class mark, it would have been enough to have printed these chief divisions of main classes in bold type.

The chief objection to the Cheltenham scheme is that it is restricted to school libraries. Pupils will find public (municipal and county) libraries classified on the Dewey system, with certain exceptions. (Some public libraries use Brown's Subject.) University libraries use either Dewey or Library of Congress. But in no case will they encounter Cheltenham when they leave school. This will make it harder for them to use other libraries than if they were used to Dewey. Another objection is that letters denote the main classes, and letters are not so simple to grasp as figures.

Enthusiasts for the Cheltenham classification will at once dismiss these objections on the ground that familiarity with one type of classification enables a pupil to grasp another speedily, and that children learn the sequence of letters by using dictionaries, while the broader base and shorter marks are a distinct advantage.

The Cheltenham classification is a very clear, sensible scheme. As the main classes are planned in accordance with the curriculum, a school library is assured of an evenly-spaced arrangement for its stock. The scheme is neither overburdened with detail, nor too broad. The notation conforms to the recognized qualities of a good classification notation—simplicity, flexibility, and brevity. There is an excellent alphabetical index of subjects, while explanatory notes have been dispersed throughout the tables to direct the classifier. There is also a useful introduction. The authors are E. S. Fegan and M. Cant; publishers, W. Heffer and Sons, Ltd., Cambridge; and the price 3s. 6d.

III. THE BLISS CLASSIFICATION

Henry Evelyn Bliss is an American philosopher and librarian who has made an intensive study of classification for about forty years. In "The organization of knowledge in libraries and the subject approach to books," he sets out his theories on library classification and outlines his own scheme. This book should be studied by anyone who intends to apply the Bliss classification to a library. "A system of bibliographic classification," containing the tables of this scheme, index, and a long explanatory introduction, was first published in 1935 by the H. W. Wilson Company, New York. The price is seven dollars.

Bliss holds very decided views on book classification and a knowledge of his chief theories is indispensable to an understanding of the scheme. He maintains that the various branches of knowledge have developed in a progressive order, now generally accepted by philosophers and educationalists, and that his order must be reproduced in a book classification.

"There are indeed two kinds of classification," he

32 CLASSIFICATION AND CATALOGUING

writes, "on the one hand the logical, natural, and scientific, on the other hand the practical, the arbitrary, the purposive; but for library classification we should join these two hands; the two purposes should be combined. To make the classification conform to the scientific and educational organization of knowledge is to make it the more practical. A logical and scientific organization of knowledge should be adapted to the practical requirements, the various bibliographic services, and the necessary economies.

Specific subjects, according to Bliss, must always be subordinate to the more general, while closely-related specific subjects must be kept near together. Alternative placings are essential in a classification, because of the varying needs of individual libraries. Notation should be simple and show the order of classes, divisions, etc., without being too long. This is a very cursory summary of Bliss's theories. The reader is recommended to study "The organization of knowledge in libraries and the subject approach to books."

The outline is worked out according to these logical principles and attempts to present knowledge in an ordered development. It starts with General works, proceeds to Philosophy; the Natural sciences; the Social sciences, including History, Religion and Applied social science; the various Arts, useful and fine; concluding with Language and Literature.

These groups of subjects are also arranged in progressive order. Bliss begins with General science, Logic,

SCHEMES FOR SCHOOL LIBRARIES 33

Mathematics, and other general methods of Science, including Metrology and Statistics. He goes on to Physics and then to Chemistry. From these fundamental sciences develop more special ones. There is Astronomy, study of the heavens. Then comes, Geology, study of the earth. It is followed by Natural history, Biology, Botany, Zoology, Anthropology (study of the highest mammal), Psychology (study of man's mind). Sixteen main classes, J to Y complete the scheme, but the above summary of A to I will show the well-planned relationships between subjects and dovetailing of one main class into the next.

At present, the scheme is only published in condensed form—that is, main classes and divisions, with an alphabetical index. Division can often be carried a stage further by the application of special tables called "systematic schedules." Some of the expanded sections may be borrowed from the Special Libraries Association, New York, but school librarians say the published scheme gives sufficient detail.

Letters are used for all main classes, except nine devoted to general works and termed "anterior numeral classes." Only the first of these, "Reference room collections," is likely to be needed. Then come classes A to Y. Z has been left blank and could be used instead of 1 for reference books. Division is by letter, except in some of the special tables. One of these, to be used under History of countries, has 3 for Topography, 4 for Antiquities. As MU is England, Travel in England

34 CLASSIFICATION AND CATALOGUING

would be MU3 and English antiquities MU4. But letters are also employed in these "systematic schedules" and often have a mnemonic value through using the initial capital letter of a subject. In Schedule 3, Constitutional history is C, Diplomatic is D, Economic E. Applying these to English we get MUC, MUD, MUE. Class marks for eight subjects in the three schemes discussed in this chapter are set out below for comparison.

Subject	*Dewey*	*Cheltenham*	*Bliss*
Bees	595·7	M73·5	GR
Climate	551·5	P4	DS
Encyclopaedias (general)	030	Z1	7I *or* I
French revolution	944	D30·4	MSN
Inorganic chemistry	546	M46	CI
Libraries (general)	020	Z14	2N
Opera (music)	782	S56	VW
Typewriting	652	C29	TJ

The scheme of Bliss is certainly very complicated and requires much study. His directions are not always clear, particularly in the use to be made of the systematic schedules, while the imitation typescript (in which the book is printed) and slanting type for instructions add to the difficulties. As far as I know, only five libraries are using the scheme—the library of the College of the City of New York, where Bliss is Associate Librarian; a university library in New Zealand; one special library and two school libraries in England. Several other school librarians are considering the scheme and possibly have begun to use it. This means that it has not yet been widely tested as a working scheme, like Dewey. Many people will also object to the notation and prefer 944 or D30·4 to a class mark like MSN; 782 or S56 to the shorter VW. A combination like MUD is certainly unfortunate.

The scheme of Bliss is unlikely to enjoy a very wide use because it has come into the field so late. No library of any size can afford the time or money to change from one classification to another, unless it has some old-fashioned scheme that is hampering its development. That criticism cannot be brought against the Decimal classification, which is continually revised and kept up to date, so "Dewey" libraries seldom consider changing to some other scheme. School libraries are much freer. Many are only facing the problem of classification for the first time, and the Bliss scheme has attracted an extraordinary amount of attention and praise from teacher-librarians. The grouping of subjects is approved. Objections are raised against the notation, but others consider any disadvantage of letters is outweighed by the general advantages of the scheme. Bliss makes a feature of alternative placings and methods of arrangement, which is very convenient. For example, Literature can be arranged in four different ways.

To quote one school librarian, Mr. C. A. Stott, "The system is scholarly, alike in its conception and in its working-out . . . it goes as far to conform with the needs of the curriculum as a system constructed on general lines can go, or as is advisable; it is admirably conceived to meet the requirements of specialist work; and its notation is economical." [1]

[1] A shorter account of classification and cataloguing will be found, together with descriptions of other aspects of school librarianship, in *School and College Library Practice*, by Monica Cant, vol. ii in this Series of Handbooks. Price 5s.

CHAPTER THREE

HOW TO APPLY A CLASSIFICATION SCHEME

THE first step towards classifying a library is the obvious, but important, task of choosing a scheme. Having made the final decision, the librarian should order at least two copies of the selected classification. One can be placed in the library for general reference. The second should be kept with other working tools (e.g. Cataloguing rules), and it is recommended that this copy be sent to a binder for interleaving and rebinding in a strong cover. Meanwhile, the librarian should make himself thoroughly familiar with the scheme. If he intends to make alterations to the tables, these can be planned and should be recorded in both copies. It is advisable to note modifications in pencil, regarding them as temporary until tested by practical experience. Readers were warned in Chapter One against the danger of giving way to enthusiasm for modifications. They should be restricted as far as possible. When made, index entries that are affected must also be altered.

Methods of working depend on whether the library is to be closed for a period while the books are classified, or whether the task has to be spread over a long period while the library remains open, and only a few days of closing allowed for final rearrangement.

In the latter case, the librarian will have to work gradually through the shelves in their present order, taking each book in turn, classifying it, and noting the number on the back of the title-page. As books on loan are returned, he must put aside unclassified ones and deal with them before they go back to the shelves. There should be a final check by the old shelf list for any that may have been missed. The librarian can also compile a new shelf list by writing out a card for each book, with the class number as the heading, and filing these in classified order. Then the library is closed and the librarian, with as many helpers as he can obtain, should record the class number of every book on the back. Directions for doing this are given later. The entire stock is arranged on the shelves according to classification marks, ample space being left on each shelf for additions. Only when the bookcases become filled and extra ones will be required, should a general move round of the stock become necessary. If plenty of gaps are left, though there have to be small moves from shelf to shelf, the space occupied for each class should be sufficient for several years. Finally, shelf guides are added and everything is ready for opening.

If a library can be closed for more than a few days, then the librarian can tackle the work in a systematic fashion. Books should be sorted roughly into main classes and arranged on the shelves according to these groups. Taking each class in turn, first re-divide into main divisions, and then into subdivisions. After this,

HOW TO APPLY A CLASSIFICATION SCHEME

start to classify each book minutely by the tables of the scheme, recording the class mark on the back of the title-page (the most permanent position) and on the back (or spine) of the cover. Arrange the books in strict classified order, leaving room for additions, write out a new shelf-list, and put up the new shelf guides.

The class number is noted in various written records, such as the catalogue, shelf-list, and accessions register. Then, it must also be put in the book itself. The most permanent and inconspicuous place is the back of the title-page. Do not write it just inside the cover, for the end-papers will be removed when the book goes for rebinding. Pencil is as clear as ink, and easier to erase if the class mark ever requires changing. The number should then be put clearly on the back of the book, starting about one and a half inches from the bottom. If the class marks appear at a fairly uniform height above the shelves, the library looks more orderly. Do not begin at the top of the book. Books are of such varying sizes that the general zigzag effect would be ludicrous.

There are three ways of marking books—by an electric pen, by white paint, and by writing on a label. The disadvantage of the electric pen is that the class mark is indelibly recorded. Even an experienced classifier has to reverse decisions occasionally, so that the beginner will be well advised to avoid an indelible method of marking. Labels wear off very soon in these days of central heating, so cannot be recommended. White paint is the most satisfactory method. The paint can be bought in sixpenny jars from a stationer's, thinned a little with water, and an ordinary pen with a fine nib used to write the mark on the book cover. A jar of paint lasts a long time, so this method is very cheap. To prevent the paint being rubbed off, or fading, it is usual to protect it with a thin coat of paper varnish. The varnish needs thinning with turpentine. It, too, can be bought in sixpenny jars from the stationer's, and is applied with a small paint-brush. The marking lasts for years and years, but can, at any time, be neatly scraped off, and alterations made.

Some system of shelf guiding is essential in an open-access library. First, there should be a plan of the library showing which subjects are allocated to the various bookcases. This can be framed and hung up in a prominent position. A large label, giving main class mark and name of this class (e.g. 700 FINE ARTS), is slipped in a holder and one placed over every case. Shelves also need guides, e.g. 720 Architecture, 821 English poetry. Shelf label-holders usually have projecting "tongues" which press against the under side of the shelf and keep the holders in place. It is then possible to move a holder along when new books are added and the contents of the shelf rearranged. Label holders for cases and shelves, and even labels to fit the holders (printed with the Dewey Decimal numbers and names of subjects), can be obtained cheaply from various commercial firms. These firms advertise in the library journals.

HOW TO APPLY A CLASSIFICATION SCHEME 41

There are three stages in classifying a book. First, the classifier has to discover the subject, next to fit the book into that subject's place in the classification scheme, and, lastly, to record the class mark inside the book, on the back, etc.

Determining the subject is not always easy and absurd mistakes can be made by the careless classifier who looks no further than the title. Many titles are plain, comprehensive statements of the book's subject, e.g. "The theory of political economy," "The butterflies of the British Isles," "The age of discovery, from Marco Polo to Henry Hudson." Others are wolves in sheeps' clothing, e.g. "The war: from the landing at Gallipoli to the death of Lord Raglan." A hasty classifier, who knows little of Lord Raglan, cheerfully puts the book at "Great War" (940·4, D21·5, MD),[1] but, fortunately, his attention is arrested by the date of publication, which is 1855. When he examines the text, he finds the subject is the Crimean war.

It is a good habit to suspect a "snag" in every book and never to classify by the title alone. Examine the list of contents, chapter headings, and, perhaps, the index. For philosophical, religious, and sociological works, one should glance through any preface, or introduction, to get the author's point of view. In the case of travel books, there are usually maps to show what countries

---

[1] Class marks in the Dewey, Cheltenham and Bliss schemes respectively. The three are given in parentheses with each example throughout this chapter.

have been visited by the author on his journey. Occasionally, one may get a book whose subject proves elusive. This may have to be read right through, or, if it has been bought in response to a colleague's suggestion, he should be consulted.

Some books are more important for the literary form in which their subject-matter is presented than for the actual subject. Usually, these are purely literary works, e.g. Milton's "Paradise lost." This is famous for its poetical form, therefore it is classified in English poetry (821, E16·0, YG), not in Religion under Fall of man (233, E22, PL). The Literature class will contain books that have literature, or types of literature, as the subject, e.g. Nicoll's "British drama: an historical survey from the beginnings to the present time," and examples of these types of literature.

Subjects viewed from special standpoints, or cast in special literary forms, must not be confused with the standpoints, or forms, themselves. There is a rule that classification should be always by subject, unless form is more important. Thus, a book of essays on British history goes in British history (942, D22, MU), not with English essays (824, E8·3, YO); but "A history of astronomy" goes in Astronomy (520, M7·1, D3), not History (900, D, LG). With titles like, "The philosophy of music," "Insurance and its law," "The evolution of decorative art," "Education as a science," "The science of law," the classifier must consider carefully and ask himself, what is the *real* subject? For whom

HOW TO APPLY A CLASSIFICATION SCHEME 43

is the book written? Is it for philosophers or for musicians? If for both, then which has the prior claim? The philosopher cannot expect books on the special applications of his subject to be in Philosophy, but the musician has a right to expect books on the philosophy of music to be in the Music section. As a general rule, the philosophy, or psychology, or law, or history of any special subject goes with that subject. General works on philosophy, psychology, law and their subdivisions are collected together, while the history of groups of people, mainly political units, form a special main class, History.

Books often deal with more than one subject. If purely general, like Cassell's "Children's book of knowledge" or Cousens' "Pros and cons," they go in the General works class. If more specific, like an encyclopaedia of science, or a collection of essays on the fine arts, they are placed in the general section of the particular main class. A safe rule is that, if a book treats of two or three specific subjects, it should be classified with the one that predominates, but if no one subject predominates, then take the first one. More than three specific subjects, equally treated, go in the more general number. Thus, a book of travel in Denmark and Holland goes at Denmark (914·89 or 948·9T,[1] P36, MO3), unless the author devotes the greater part

[1] 914·89 is according to the Dewey table, but, as explained in Chapter Two, there is a recognized modification which puts Travel with History and adds a distinguishing T. The history of Denmark is simply 948·9.

of the text to Holland, when the class mark for that country should be chosen (914·92 or 949·2T, P31·2, MP3). Supposing the book covers Denmark, Holland, Germany, and Poland, then put it at the general number for European travel (914 or 940T, P21, M3). When we have a book describing the influence of one subject on another, like "The influence of Icelandic sagas upon English literature" or "Tennyson and Virgil: an essay on the indebtedness of Tennyson to Virgil," the rule is to classify with the subject or author influenced.

If a book is written in a foreign language, this does not affect the classification. A French book on architecture is classified in Architecture, not in French language; a German scientific treatise in Science, not in German language; and so on. Translations should stand with the originals, and so should criticisms, keys, analyses, commentaries, etc.

The second stage in classifying is to fit the book into its appropriate place in the classification. The Dewey, Cheltenham, and Bliss schemes are equipped with alphabetical subject indexes, so that specific subjects can be found quickly in the tables. An index is a useful tool, but must not be depended upon for classifying. Many subjects belong to more than one place, according to treatment. For example, one may have books on the subject Gold scattered amongst Chemistry (chemical composition of the metal), Geology (distribution of gold ores), Money (economics of gold), Numismatics (study of gold coins), and so on. Thus, it is important that the classifier should always turn to the tables and see that the book fits into its right division and main class, as well as in a place for the specific subject.

The classifier must endeavour to be impartial in his decisions. This is difficult for the specialist, who tends to collect everything pertaining to his subject in that class, whether it fairly belongs there, or not. The English literature master wants all Ruskin's work put in Literature, although many of them are contributions to other branches of knowledge. "The seven lamps of architecture" and "The stones of Venice" belong to Architecture. "Modern painters" should go in Painting, "Unto this last" in Economics, and "Queen of the air" in Mythology. Remember, an author's complete works can be traced by means of the Author catalogue, so do not try to make Classification undertake the functions of another library tool.

Another golden rule is to classify as minutely as the scheme allows and the stock demands. Do not place a book like "England under the Tudors" at 942, D22, MU. It is lost among all the works dealing with the whole of English history, and there will be several shelves of these. Give it its period subdivision (942·05, D22·5, MVF or MVG[1]), and collect all books dealing specifically with the Tudors there, separated from their predecessors, the Houses of Lancaster and York

---

[1] Bliss has two divisions for the Tudor period. MVF would be the better place for this book.

(942·04, D22·4, MVE), and followed by the Stuarts (942·06, D22·6, MVH).

If a subject arises that has no place in the scheme, make a place for it and record your decision in the index, as well as in the tables.

Collected works and series are a problem. As a rule these should be separated under their respective subjects. It is certainly inadvisable to keep a series, like English men of letters or Loeb classical library, intact, but volumes making up one work, like the Cambridge modern history, should stand together at the general number of the class or division. Collected works of writers like Ruskin cannot always be broken up. A library may unfortunately possess a set where a separate work finishes half-way through a volume and another begins, so that it is physically impossible to break it up. There is a place for such "complete or partial collections of an author's work, treating of various subjects" at 081 in Dewey, Z3 in Cheltenham, and 7 in Bliss.

The ideal arrangement for a classified library is in strict order of the classification scheme, e.g. 000 to 999 of Dewey, A to Z of Cheltenham, 1 to Y of Bliss, but, for reasons of space saving, very large books (i.e. those twelve inches in height and over) will have to be removed from the general sequence and shelved together. There is no reason why they should not also be in classified order on these "oversize" shelves. Most librarians like to keep reference works (i.e. books that cannot be taken out of the library) together, which may make a third "parallel classification." Maps, pamphlets, etc., should be put in subject boxes. The number required depends on the amount of material. A library with four pamphlets on scientific subjects can put these in one box and shelve it at the general class mark for science. If there are twenty, then boxes for the separate divisions —Physics, Chemistry, Botany, etc.—will be needed. Fiction and Junior books will probably be kept on separate shelves. The Cheltenham scheme provides special main classes for these.

Although certain rules have been given in this chapter, it is realized that librarians may wish to modify some of them because of individual curriculum demands. Here the classifier must use his discretion, remembering that convenience governs all placings. School libraries exist for teachers and pupils, and the books are purchased in response to teaching and study requirements. So long as one section is not starved at the expense of another, there is no harm in the librarian classifying a book in a section that needs it, although, theoretically, it belongs elsewhere. Translations should stand with the originals, but if Pope's "Translation of Homer's Iliad" is not wanted in Classics and is wanted in English literature, this rule should then be broken. Sometimes, duplication is the only solution. More's "Utopia" should properly be classed under "Ideal States" in Political science, but a second copy can be purchased for Literature, if the

English master particularly wants it in that section. The librarian, however, must beware of giving way to individual demands when the balance of the library is likely to be upset. Specialists are apt to be biased in favour of the claims of their own subjects, and here the librarian stands as co-ordinating officer and impartial judge.

CHAPTER FOUR

KINDS OF CATALOGUES. DISPLAY. MAKE-UP OF ENTRY

THE catalogue is often termed an index to the library's contents, as its primary function is to show where books can be found. Besides the purpose of location, the catalogue may also include detailed descriptions of books, showing minute differences between one copy and another. This side of cataloguing only becomes important in libraries that stock old and rare books. In the school library, attention is concentrated on the catalogue as a finding list, rather than a bibliographical tool. Therefore, only enough description need be given to identify a particular work.

KINDS OF CATALOGUES

Catalogues fall roughly into three groups, according to the ways of finding a book. A reader may want a book by a particular author. He may have fogotten the author's name, but remember the title. He may want any book dealing with a particular subject, or written in a particular literary form.

In an Author catalogue, entries are made under the names of authors, these being arranged in alphabetical sequence. In the Title catalogue, some word from a book's title, usually the first unless an article, is selected as heading. A Subject catalogue enters books under subjects—or, forms, if more important. It may use the specific name of a subject as heading, e.g. "The origin of earthquakes" under EARTHQUAKES: this is known as the Alphabetical-Subject catalogue. The Alphabetical-Classed takes the name of the group, or class, with specific subject as sub-heading, e.g. GEOLOGY—Earthquakes. In the Classified, the class mark is the heading. Thus, if Dewey is used, earthquakes are represented by 551; if Cheltenham, P3; if Bliss, DH.

The Classified catalogue must always stand alone, since its headings cannot be combined with purely alphabetical ones. Libraries having this variety need, in addition, Author and Title catalogues. The latter are often combined, forming a single file, and some libraries prefer to add subject entries for books about people—i.e. under names of biographies, etc. When these personal subject entries are added, the Author-and-title catalogue becomes a Name catalogue. Thus, "Greatheart of Papua," by W. P. Nairne, the story of a famous missionary called James Chalmers, would have an entry under the author, NAIRNE; under the first word of the title, GREATHEART; and under the name of the individual who forms the subject, CHALMERS.

Instead of Classified and Name catalogues, some libraries prefer the Dictionary catalogue. This consists of author, title, and specific subject entries, arranged in one sequence. "At the turn of the tide," by Richard

KINDS OF CATALOGUES, ETC. 51

Perry, deals with birds. The author entry would be under PERRY, title entry under AT, and subject entry under BIRDS. Often, author and title entries are kept in one file and there is a separate Alphabetical-subject, or an Alphabetical-classed catalogue.

All these catalogues will be discussed more fully in subsequent chapters.

METHODS OF DISPLAY

Some flexible form of display, whereby entries can be added indefinitely at any place, is essential in a growing library. It is not practical to use exercise books as entries will have to be rewritten when there is no longer room to insert new ones. The card and the sheaf are the two more practical forms.

The sheaf consists of slips which fit into binders, on the loose-leaf principle. One entry is made per page, and the slips can be removed and new ones inserted. This form is popular because it is easy to use and carbon copies of entries can be made, thus lightening the task of writing added entries.

The type of catalogue that has universal approval is the card form, an entry for every book being made on a separate card. Cards are cut to the standard size of $7\frac{1}{2}$ by $12\frac{1}{2}$ cm. and of varying thicknesses. "Medium weight" is best, as too thick cards fill up the catalogue drawers too quickly, and thin ones bend easily and soon wear out. Commercial firms supply cards, ruled and unruled, with a punched hole through which a drawer rod can run.

Cabinets are made with drawers to hold the cards. Each drawer has a block of wood that holds the cards erect. A locking rod keeps them from being removed, except by releasing a special control, while an automatic stop prevents the drawer from being pulled right out of its place, and perhaps accidentally overturned. The contents of a drawer are shown by a label on the outside and by guide cards inside. Guide cards have projecting tabs and are inserted among the catalogue entries; there is usually one to about fifty entry cards.

MAKE-UP OF AN ENTRY

The first part of a catalogue entry is the heading. As explained, this may be the name of the author, a word from the title, or description of the subject. All depends on the type of catalogue. Entries are arranged by their headings, that is, alphabetically, except in the Classified catalogue where the order will follow the notation of the classification scheme. Rules for choosing headings are given in Chapters V to VIII.

Next comes a description of the book. This covers the title, details concerning publication and make-up.

The title of the book should be transcribed from the title-page, not from the cover—unless the copy is imperfect and its title-page missing. The full title includes the name of the author and statement of edition, if other than the first.

E.g. Wireless: the modern magic carpet, by Ralph Stranger. Third edition.

The explanatory part, following the concise title or name of the book, is called the subtitle, and it is permissible to omit unessential parts of this.

E.g. The romance of submarine engineering: containing interesting descriptions in non-technical language of the construction of submarine boats, the salving of great ships, the recovery of sunken treasure, the building of breakwaters and docks, and many other feats of engineering beneath the surface of the water, by T. W. Corbin.

This can be cut down to "The romance of submarine engineering." Parts of the subtitle, necessary to an understanding of the main title, should be given.

E.g. The pageant of civilization: world romance and adventures as told by postage stamps.

In an Author catalogue, the name of the author appears in the heading, so many libraries omit it from the title. This is quite permissible unless the form of name on the title-page differs from the form used in the heading, e.g. pseudonymous writers. Full explanations of such cases are given in Chapter Five. Phrases noting editor or translator are important and must be included.

54 CLASSIFICATION AND CATALOGUING

Information about the edition may appear on the title-page, on the back of the title-page, or in some other part of the book, possibly the preface or introduction. Unless otherwise stated, first edition is assumed. This need not be given, but "second edition" or "revised edition," etc., imply changes in the text and are particularly important for scientific and technical works. If the library has two editions of the same work, each should be catalogued separately. Edition is regarded as part of the full title.

E.g. A textbook of physiology. Third edition, revised.

> A Greek grammar for schools, based on the principles and requirements of the Grammatical Society. Part I —Accidence. Seventh edition.

It will be noticed that capital letters are only used for names of persons, societies, languages, and after a period. They would also be given for places, names of any corporate bodies, and wherever customary usage decreed. but they should not be used for ordinary nouns. The safest rule is to keep down capitals to a minimum. The entry then looks more natural and is easier to read.

Punctuation should follow that of the title-page. When none is given, which is frequently the case, the cataloguer must supply it. Certain conventions have grown up over punctuation. A colon is generally used to separate a subtitle from the principal title, e.g. "The

KINDS OF CATALOGUES, ETC.

golden fleece: an introduction to the industrial history of England." Square brackets indicate additions made by the cataloguer, e.g. "The golden staircase: [poems]."

At the bottom of the title-page will be found the name of the publisher, place of publication, and date. These items are termed the Imprint. Date should always be given. If it does not appear on the front of the title-page, it may be on the back. Failing this, it may be at the end of the preface. But, whenever possible, the exact or an approximate date ought to be found, and n.d. (abbreviation for no date) only be given as a last resort. Place of publication may certainly be omitted. Most school librarians find it convenient to record the name of the publisher, maintaining it is useful when ordering new copies, checking, etc. Leave a space of nearly half an inch between title and imprint, so that the division between the two is marked.

E.g.   The golden age. Second edition.   Lane, 1895.

The items which constitute the physical make-up of a book are called the Collation. Collation consists of the number of pages, or volumes (if more than one), details of illustrations, and the height of the book. Items must be given in this order and various abbreviations are used.

E.g.   vi, 191p.   fronts. pls. ports. facsims.   24 cm.

Such detail is not necessary in a open-access library where books can be readily examined. Pagination can be ignored, but if a work is in more than one volume, the number of volumes must be given, e.g. 2v. It may also be useful to state whether or not a book is illustrated. Size can be omitted. If a book is so large that it has to go on special shelves, a note may be added, or a distinguishing letter like q (i.e. quarto) placed before the class mark.

Collation is followed by the name of the series, provided the book belongs to one. This is given in parenthesis. Finally, there comes the location mark, which, in a classified library, is the class mark. This should be placed in the top right-hand corner (except in the Classified catalogue, where it is part of the heading), above the heading. The accessions number goes at the bottom of the card.

Examples of entries are given below. These are for an Author catalogue. Dewey (abridged) class marks have been given, and the position of the accessions number indicated. If cards are ruled (as shown in Example 1) with a line 1 cm. from the top, and two margins on the left-hand side, each 1 cm. to the left, this will guide the cataloguer in beginning heading and and title at the same place, and make the catalogue look uniform.

Example 1.—Subtitle. Book has no series. Is not illustrated.

	571
AULT, Norman.	
Life in ancient Britain: a survey of the social and economic development of the people of England from earliest times to the Roman conquest. Longmans, 1920.	
	Acc. No.

Example 2.—Belongs to a series. Is illustrated.

551·5

BRUNT, David.

Meteorology. Oxford University Press, 1928. Illus. (World's manuals)

Acc. No.

Example 3.—Title must include phrase "edited by . . ."

938

GROTE, George.

A history of Greece from the time of Solon to 403 B.C.; condensed and edited by J. M. Mitchell and M. O. B. Caspari. Routledge, 1930.

Acc. No.

Example 4.—Work in more than one volume

            821
 NOYES, Alfred.
   The torch-bearers. Blackwood, 1922–30.
3v.
           Acc. No.

CHAPTER FIVE

THE AUTHOR AND TITLE CATALOGUE—AUTHOR ENTRIES

THE primary purpose of the Author catalogue is to answer the questions, Have you a certain book by So-and-so? and, What books have you by So-and-so? To answer these, all works by a single author must be collected in the catalogue under one form of his name.

Authors fall into two groups, individual and corporate. Individual authors are by far the more common. Usually a single writer has brought the book into being, e.g. "Pickwick papers, by Charles Dickens." But there may be two, or more, individuals collaborating, e.g. "Getting one's living, by Gerard Fiennes and L. G. Pilkington." When governments, societies, etc., issue publications, authorship is termed "corporate," since the corporate body is primarily responsible for the book's existence, and thus the author. A catalogue of the British Museum is entered under "British Museum," the Library Association year book under "Library Association."

In the majority of cases of individual authorship, entry is made under the surname, followed by any Christian names. A comma separates Christian names from the surname, which is often put in block capitals to make the alphabetical filing of the catalogue cards easier. Christian names should be given in full, blanks being left after initials until the names can be discovered. Supposing the title-page reads, "Doctor Barnado: physician, pioneer, prophet, by J. Wesley Bready." Author heading would be,

        BREADY, J   Wesley.

If the author publishes a later work and signs himself as James or John, the Christian name can be put in the blank left in the first entry, making it identical with the new one. Such consistency is very important. Authors who first use initials and later full names may otherwise get their works separated as the catalogue grows. If only initials are given throughout, then authors with the same surnames and initials, e.g. all the J. Smiths, will be mixed up together. It must never be forgotten that the main purpose of the Author catalogue is to show what works the library possesses by different authors and to collect under each author the titles of the works he has written. Even if the catalogue is too small for works by authors of the same names and initials to get mixed, because these are so few, nothing looks worse than a variety of headings for the same writer. A library possessing several works by the late Sir Ernest Wallis Budge, had entries under the following headings—a result of slack cataloguing:

BUDGE, E. A. W.
BUDGE, E. A. Wallis.
BUDGE, Ernest A. T. Wallis.
BUDGE, *Sir* Ernest A. T. Wallis.
BUDGE, *Sir* Ernest Alfred T. Wallis.
BUDGE, *Sir* Ernest Alfred Thompson Wallis.

Difficulties constantly arise in individual author entry, owing to the vagaries of writers. Some authors use fictitious names, as well as their real ones; some have surnames in two or three parts; some have no surnames at all. In many cases it is not easy to decide who really is the author of a particular work.

Every school librarian should own an interleaved copy of the Anglo-American code of cataloguing rules, commonly called the Joint code. The full title is "Cataloguing rules: author and title entries. Compiled by committees of the Library Association and of the American Library Association." The price is 6s. to members of the Library Association and 7s. 6d. to non-members. This code is very detailed and contains exceptional cases as well as the more common ones. The fifteen rules given at the end of this chapter will be found sufficient for ordinary practice. Rules for Change of name and Noblemen follow the American alternatives, and No. 9, Pseudonyms, the Library of Congress rule. Otherwise, the rules conform with the English edition of the A.A. code, but a copy of the code should be available for reference when exceptional cases occur.

The general rule is that a book by an individual author should be entered under the surname, followed by any Christian names. (Rule 1.)

   E.g. LEE, Herbert Patrick.

Many authors have hyphenated surnames, like Baring-Gould, Sackville-West, Watts-Dunton, and the question arises, under which part of the compound should they be entered? Some readers will go to West for Victoria Sackville-West, but the majority are more likely to look under Sackville-West. In such cases, entry under the first half is preferred, this being the practice of the Dictionary of national biography, "Who's who," and other important reference works. There should be some direction from the half (or other parts) not used. (Rule 2.)

E.g. *Entry card*
   HAIG-BROWN, R   L

    Silver: the life story of an Atlantic salmon. Black, 1931. Illus.

Reference card
   BROWN, R   L   Haigh-
    see
   HAIG-BROWN, R   L

This "direction" or reference is not a catalogue entry, but a guide from a rejected heading to the one used. Its message is, "Nothing here. Look somewhere else."

When writing a reference on a card, the rejected heading should be indented and the accepted heading moved outwards, so that it readily catches the eye. Do not record the book's title or any other details. This is a direction from one *heading* to another, and the card will serve for all cases of the use of that heading, i.e. *all* books by that author. The library may have four books by Victoria Sackville-West entered under Sackville-West that is, four cards with that heading. But it will only need a single reference card under West, Victoria Sackville-.

Christian names used with surnames, like John Stuart Mill, are not regarded as forming compound surnames. David Lloyd George and Arthur Conan Doyle are entered under George and Doyle, not Lloyd George or Conan Doyle.

Another type of compound surname is one involving a prefix, like De la Mare. Whether entry should be made under the prefix or not depends on nationality. The part of the name following is used in all but the following cases—and these exceptions account for a great number of books in an English library. First, we enter under the prefix when it is written as one word with the surname, e.g. Delafield, Macdonald. Secondly, all English and American authors are entered under the prefix, but French writers only when it consists of, or contains, an article. Italian and Spanish names go under the prefix only when it is an article. (Rule 3.)

Examples

    General rule.   BRINK, Jan ten.
                            GOETHE, Johann Wolfgang von.

Exceptions

(1) Forming one word.
        DESCARTES, René.

(2) English
        DE LA MARE, Walter.
        LE FEUVRE, Amy.
        VAN LOON, H   W

(3) French
        DU MUSSET, Alfred.
        LA FONTAINE, Jean de.
        LE SAGE, Alain René.
        (*but* VIGNY, Alfred de.)

(4) Italian and Spanish
        LI GOTTI
        LO GATTO
        (*but* GAMA, Vasco da.)

Authors who change their names are a trial to cataloguers. The majority are married women, who sometimes publish first under the maiden name and then under the married one. They may use their own Christian names or initials, or their husbands'. The American and English committees who drew up the Anglo-American code could not agree over the entry of such authors, and alternative rules are provided. The English one is very rigid, prescribing entry under the name first used as an author, with reference from later ones. This puts Elizabeth Barrett Browning under Barrett, since she published her first work in 1826 and did not marry until 1846. Mrs. Gaskell is entered under Gaskell, not Stevenson, since she never wrote under her maiden name. School libraries will probably find it better to adopt the American alternative rule, which prescribes entry under the latest name, unless an earlier is decidedly better known. This puts both Elizabeth Barrett Browning and Mrs. Gaskell under their married names, but leaves Charlotte Brontë under Brontë, not Nicholls. (Rule 4.)

Some married women use their own Christian names, e.g. Margaret Isabel Cole. Others adopt their husband's full name, or his surname and initials. In these cases, the title "Mrs." must be inserted to distinguish such a writer from her husband, while a reference may be needed from the married surname and own Christian names, as well as from her former surname, if it has been used for authorship purposes.

E.g. WEBB, *Mrs.* Sidney.

References should be made from:

(1) WEBB, Beatrice.
(2) POTTER, Beatrice.

Titles are somewhat perplexing to the beginner. Ordinary titles of address, such as Mr., ecclesiastical titles below the rank of bishop, military, naval, academic and professional titles, are all omitted in catalogue headings. Very large libraries may occasionally include them for the purpose of distinguishing two people of the same name, and, as explained in the previous paragraph, "Mrs." may be used to separate the writings of husband and wife. Titles appearing before the Christian names are capitalized and always underlined, so as not to affect the indexing. A card with the heading, WEBB, Mrs. Sidney, is to be filed directly after WEBB, Sidney, not between WEBB, Mary and WEBB, Monica. In printed catalogues, titles between surnames and Christian names were italicized, and the same kind of type used for titles that followed the Christian names. Hence the general custom of underlining all titles of honour, although it is not strictly necessary for those coming at the end of headings.

There are certain courtesy titles given to children of English noblemen. Younger sons of dukes and marquesses have the title "lord." This must be inserted before the Christian name, e.g. "Lord Eustace Percy," "Lord George Scott," "Lord Charles Cavendish." In a catalogue author heading, the surname is put first,

> E.g. PERCY, *Lord* Eustace.

Younger sons of earls, and sons of viscounts and barons, are termed "honourable."

> E.g. FINCH-HATTON, *Hon.* Harold.

Daughters of dukes, marquesses, and earls have the

title "lady," and those of viscounts and barons, "honourable."

  E.g. BENTINCK, *Lady* Norah.

Lady Norah was the daughter of the Earl of Gainsborough. "Right honourable," which belongs to peers, members of the Privy Council, and cabinet ministers, is not inserted in the heading. The "Sir" before the christian name of a baronet or knight is given.

  E.g. SCOTT, *Sir* Walter.

 The title "lord" is commonly applied to all members of the English peerage, except dukes, but, unlike the courtesy title used by younger sons of dukes and marquesses, it is never put before the Christian names. We have Alfred, Lord Tennyson, *not* Lord Alfred Tennyson; Lord Macaulay, *not* Lord Thomas Babington Macaulay. The same applies to wives of peers, baronets and knights, who are "lady." Unless they have the courtesy title, a privilege confined to daughters of dukes, marquesses, and earls, the "lady" comes after the Christian names. For example, we have Ethel Gwendoline, Lady Vincent; Augusta, Lady Gregory; but Lady Mary Wortley Montagu was the daughter of a duke, so she is Lady Mary, not Lady Montagu. These names appear in catalogue headings:

  E.g. VINCENT, Ethel Gwendoline, *lady*.
    GREGORY, Augusta, *lady*.
    MONTAGU, *Lady* Mary Wortley.

Titles following names are not capitalized in headings.

It is permissible to enter Tennyson as TENNYSON Alfred, *lord*, but rather slack cataloguing. The full title should be given.

E.g. TENNYSON, Alfred, *1st baron Tennyson*.

Noblemen are troublesome in catalogues because they may be known either by the family name or by the title. In the case of Tennyson, Macaulay, etc., the two are identical, but more often they are different and a choice has to be made. Noblemen sign by their titles, e.g. "By the Earl of Dunraven." The majority are better known by title, but there are some outstanding exceptions, e.g. Francis Bacon (first Viscount St. Albans), Horace Walpole (fourth earl of Orford), and John Buchan (first baron Tweedsmuir). Authors often publish under the family name before succeeding to a title, and then publish under the title. For example, Algernon B. Freeman-Mitford wrote a book "Tales of old Japan," but copies published after he became Baron Redesdale have on the title-page "By Lord Redesdale," and give no indication of his full name. The English rule in the Anglo-American code follows British Museum practice and enjoins entry under family name, with reference from title. This puts Lord Chesterfield under Stanhope, Lord Nuffield under Morris. Here again, school librarians will probably prefer the American alternative, which orders entry to be made under the latest title, unless a nobleman is much better known by an earlier one, or by his family name. References must be made from rejected headings (Rule 5). In such references, both used and rejected headings must be given in full so that there can be no confusion. "Chesterfield *see* Stanhope, Philip Dormer" is absurd. Give titles fully and correctly, as shown in the following examples.

E.g. *Entry card*

[1]910

    BUCHAN, John, *1st baron Tweedsmuir.*

       A book of escapes and hurried journeys. Nelson, 1927.

Reference card

    TWEEDSMUIR, John Buchan, *1st baron*
       see
    BUCHAN, John, *1st baron Tweedsmuir.*

Wives of noblemen are subject to the same rules, and also come under the rule for "Change of name."

A bishop or an archbishop is entered under the surname, with the title following any Christian names. There should be a reference from the name of the see.

E.g. *Entry card*

323

    MASTERMAN, J   Howard B   *bp. of Plymouth.*

       The House of Commons: its place in national history. Murray, 1908.

[1] Dewey class marks given in this and subsequent examples.

Reference card

        PLYMOUTH, J   Howard B   Masterman, *bp. of*

    see
    MASTERMAN, J   Howard B   *bp. of Plymouth.*

Archbishops often omit their surnames from title-pages, so care should be taken, e.g. "By Edward White, archbishop." A glance at the cover shows that the book is by Archbishop Benson, and the heading should be BENSON, Edward White, *abp. of Canterbury*.

Popes, saints, sovereigns, and early writers known only by forenames are to be entered under forenames, e.g. Thomas à Kempis (Rule 7). English sovereigns are described as king (or queen) of England until 1603. After that, Great Britain is substituted for England, e.g. JAMES I, *king of Great Britain*. This coincides with the use of the headings "England" and "Great Britain" for government publications in corporate entry.

Classical writers should be entered under the full Latin form (Rule 8).

E.g. HOMERUS.
      TACITUS, Caius Cornelius.
      VERGILIUS MARO, Publius.   Reference from
                                                  VIRGIL.

Pseudonymous writers fall into two groups. There are those who consistently write under one assumed name and are better known by that than by the real one, e.g. George Eliot. The second group writes partly under the real name and partly under one or more pseudonyms. It also includes writers who are well known under the true name. The A.A. code is too rigid for a school library, since its rule orders entry under the real name whenever this can be found. Such a rule works quite well for Charlotte Brontë, who is not so well known under her pseudonym of Currer Bell, but it puts George Eliot's books under Evans, Mary Ann. A better plan is to enter under best-known name (Rule 9).

E.g. *Entry card*
    BRONTË, Emily.
        Wuthering heights, by Ellis Bell, *pseud*.
    Collins, 1937.

Reference card
    BELL, Ellis, *pseud*.
        see
    BRONTË, Emily.

E.g. *Entry card*
    CARROLL, Lewis, *pseud*.
        Alice's adventures in wonderland.
    Macmillan, 1899. Illus.

Reference card
    DODGSON, Charles Lutwidge
        see
    CARROLL, Lewis, *pseud*.

No school library is likely to have copies of the mathematical works of this author, published under his real name. If they did, a decision would have to be made concerning the choice of heading, and all books entered under Carroll or Dodgson, regardless of the name used on the title-page. The name on the title-page, if it differs from the heading, should be included in the title.

Up to now, we have considered entry under one form or name, with necessary references. As explained, the reference card should not contain details of title, etc. It merely directs the reader from one heading to another. Consequently, only one reference card is needed under each of the rejected headings. A third type of card is the added, or secondary entry. This is similar to the usual "main" entry, but has an additional heading. In an author catalogue it is made for individuals who may have added something or collaborated with the author.

An editor may take the position of "author" and the main entry be made under his name. This is when he alone is responsible for the compilation, although he may not have actually written the entire text. For example, Francis Palgrave is regarded as "author" of "The golden treasury," Robert Bridges of "The Chilswell book of English poetry." The abbreviation "ed." is added after his name in the heading. But we also have cases of author and editor, e.g. "La morte d'Arthur, by Sir Thomas Malory; edited by Sir Edward Strachey." Strachey has modernized the edition and

THE AUTHOR AND TITLE CATALOGUE 73

furnished it with notes, glossary, and index. Main entry should be under Malory, and then an additional entry under Strachey (Rule 10).

Added entries are also made for translators, the abbreviation *tr.* following his name. Main entry for a translation must always be under the original author. The same rule applies to epitomes, retold versions, abridgments, etc. (Rule 10).

The added entry heading is put above the original main entry heading and indented 1 cm.

E.g. *Main entry*

                                                    883
HOMERUS.

    The Odyssey; translated into English in the original metre, by Francis Caulfield. G. Bell, 1923.   (Bohn's popular library)

Added entry

    CAULFIELD, Francis, *tr.*   883
HOMERUS.

    The Odyssey; translated into English in the original metre, by Francis Caulfield. G. Bell, 1923   (Bohn's popular library)

A record of all added entries and references should be made on the back of the main entry card. This is merely for the cataloguer's private reference. If alterations are to be made or books withdrawn, this record ensures that no cards have been overlooked. The headings recorded are termed "tracings." For example, "Stories from the Aeneid; retold from Virgil in simple language by Alfred J. Church" would have main entry under VERGILIUS MARO, Publius; added entry under CHURCH, Alfred J   ; and a reference from VIRGIL. The tracings on the back of the main entry card would be:

Added entries
        CHURCH, Alfred J

References
        VIRGIL *see*

When there are two authors, it is customary to give the names of both in the main entry heading.

E.g.

                                        575
    GEDDES, Patrick, *and* Thomson, J   Arthur.
        Evolution. Butterworth, 1928. (Home university library of modern knowledge)

There will be an added entry.

            THOMSON, J   Arthur, *jt. author*. 575
      GEDDES, Patrick, *and* Thomson, J   Arthur.
          Evolution. Butterworth, 1928. (Home university library of modern knowledge)

If more than two, the heading is the name of the first author, followed by the words, *and others*, and the names of the other authors are given in the title or in a note. An added entry is made for each author, other than the first (Rule 11).

Corporate authorship can only be touched on very briefly. Rules are given for the four chief groups (Rules 12 to 15). Corporate bodies are divided into three kinds, governments, societies, institutions. Government publications may be national and local. If national, the name of the department, etc., concerned is given as a sub-heading.

E.g.
>GREAT Britain. Board of Education.

Local publications go under the name of the local governing body. Then there are learned and other societies, where entry is made directly under the name of the society.

E.g.
>ZOOLOGICAL Society of London.

Institutions include universities, churches, libraries, museums, art galleries, etc. The exact specification of what is included in the term will be found on page 24 of the A.A. code. Most publications issued by institutions are entered under place, with name of the body as sub-heading, but some go directly under name. Rule 14 states the general rule, and Rule 15 name entry, but for special cases the A.A. code must be consulted. The majority of school libraries get very few cases of corporate entry, so it seems out of place to deal with the subject more fully here. If more detail is required, the librarian is referred to the A.A. code and to Sharp's textbook on cataloguing, Chapter VI.[1]

RULES for author entry

A *Individual authorship*

1. *General.*—Enter a work of individual authorship under the name of the author. The surname should come first, followed by any Christian name.

2. *Compound surnames.*—When an author has a compound surname, enter under the first part, making references from any other parts.

3. *Surnames with prefixes.*—Enter generally under the part of the name following the prefix, except:
   (1) When the prefix and name are written as one word.
   (2) When the author is British or American.
   (3) For French authors when the prefix consists of or contains an article.
   (4) For Italian and Spanish authors when the prefix is an article.

4. *Change of name, including married women.*—Enter a writer who changes his or her name, under the best-known form, with reference from any other form used for authorship. The title "Mrs'" is to be inserted between sur-

[1] Sharp, Henry A. "Cataloguing." Grafton, 1937. Price 18s. 6d.

name and Christian names to distinguish a married woman from her husband when she uses his Christian name or initials.

5. *Noblemen.*—Enter a nobleman under his latest title, unless he is better known by an earlier title or by his family name. Make references from the family name, and/or titles not used as entry word.

6. *Bishops and archbishops.*—Enter a bishop or archbishop under the surname, unless included in Rule 7, and make reference from the name of the see.

7. *Writers known by forenames.*—Enter writers known only by their forenames, e.g. popes, saints, sovereigns, and early writers, under the forenames.

8. *Ancient Greek and Latin writers.*—Enter classical writers under the full Latin forms of their names.

9. *Pseudonymous writers.*—If the real name of a pseudonymous writer is known, enter under the real name, but if the writer has written consistently under one pseudonym and is much better known by that, prefer entry under the pseudonym. Make a reference either from the pseudonym or real name.

10. *Editors, translators, etc.*—While the main entry is made under the author of a work, there should also be an added, or secondary, entry under the editor, translator, or reviser, etc.

11. *Several authors.*—Enter a work by two or more authors under the first, with added entry under each of the others. The names of all should be given in the title, or in a note.

B *Corporate authorship*

12. *Government publications.*—Enter publications of governments (national and local) under the country, county, town, or district. Give the name of the department, committee, etc., as sub-heading.

13. *Societies.*—Enter the publications of a society under the name of the society, with reference from the place where its headquarters are situated (if considered necessary).

14. *Institutions.*—Enter the publications of an institution under the name of the place where it is situated, with the name of the institution as sub-heading.

15. *Institutions whose names begin with a proper name or adjective.*—When an institution has a name beginning with a proper name or adjective, its name, not the name of the place, is used as entry word, and a reference made from place. This rule does not apply to colleges, etc., of a university; churches, monasteries, etc.; or, public libraries.

CHAPTER SIX

THE AUTHOR AND TITLE CATALOGUE—
TITLE ENTRIES

LIKE author entry, title entry may be main or added (i.e. secondary). The main entry in an Author and Title catalogue should be under author (individual or corporate) whenever possible, while an added entry may be made under title. There are certain books, however, that have no author and then main entry has to be title.

Before discussing rules for title entry, it is necessary to emphasize the importance of the actual entry-word, as the catalogue card will be filed under this. In individual authorship, obviously alphabetical arrangement must be by surname, except for writers only known by a forename or pseudonym. Thus, the surname is always put first in a heading and regarded as the entry word. Block capitals emphasize its position and help in filing. They should also be used to indicate a forename or pseudonym standing in place of a surname.

E.g.
  BENIANS, Sylvia.
  ELIOT, George, *pseud*.
  KING-HALL, Stephen.
  THOMAS *à Kempis*.

In title-entry, some word from the title must be selected, and usually stands alone in the heading. The difficulty of taking the "most important" word, is that cataloguers and readers may differ in their choice. Is the reader going to look under "fair" or "maid" or "Perth" for "The fair maid of Perth"? "The Swiss family Robinson" is a book whose title is often better remembered than the author's name. Should it have added title entry under "Swiss" or "family" or "Robinson"? As a general rule, it is better to keep to the first word, excluding articles. "The fair maid of Perth" would then be entered under "fair" and the "Swiss family Robinson" under "Swiss." Exceptions may be made for certain well-known novels, where the beginning of the title is usually dropped (Rule 16). For example, "The posthumous papers of the Pickwick Club," "The adventures of Oliver Twist," and "The expedition of Humphry Clinker" are better entered under "Pickwick," "Oliver," and "Humphry" rather than "posthumous," "adventures," or "expedition." But "The ordeal of Richard Feverel" should have "ordeal" as the entry word, since the full title of this book is generally known.

Added title entry is made whenever a book is likely to be asked for under title. This applies particularly to works of imaginative literature, such as drama, fiction, where an author's name may be forgotten, but the title remembered. There are also cases of striking titles in other classes, e.g. "Seven pillars of wisdom," "Unto this last."

These entries should not be made unnecessarily. Do

not make them for titles like "Complete works," "Collected plays," "Selected essays," since no one would require the complete works of an author whose name he did not know. When the author's name is known, the book can be located by means of the author entry. Many titles express subject, e.g. "Stories of scientific discovery," "A social and industrial history of England," "Elements of musical appreciation." Here again, title entry is superfluous. If the author's name has been forgotten, the book can be traced in the subject catalogue or found in its classified place on the shelf (Rule 17).

Title entry is set out like any other added entry.

E.g. *Main entry*

                                                  821

    KIPLING, Rudyard.

        The seven seas.   Methuen, 1929.

Added entry

        SEVEN.   821
    KIPLING, Rudyard.

        The seven seas.   Methuen, 1929.

An anonymous work is one in which the author's name does not appear anywhere in the book. Sometimes it is omitted from the title-page, but may be given at the end of the preface or introduction. There may be a biographical note contributed by someone else in which his identity is disclosed. Failing information in the book itself, it is often possible to discover the author from another library catalogue or from the standard reference work, Halkett and Laing's "Dictionary of anonymous and pseudonymous literature."[1] When the author has been found, entry is made under his name, while it is advisable to make an added entry for the title.

When the author cannot be traced, the main entry must be under title (Rule 18). Here again, the rule of "first word, excluding articles" should be followed. The heading, like a main author entry, begins at the first, not the second margin on the catalogue card.

E.g.

                                                                                            243

    GREAT.

        The great secret: being the letters of an old man to a young woman. Watts. 1911.

The distinction between pseudonymous and anonymous literature is rather a fine one. A pseudonym is an assumed name, e.g. Anatole France, Fiona Macleod, Gilcraft, Boz, Alpha of the Plough, and in such cases entry is made under the real name or the pseudonym (*see* Rule 9). But typographical devices, e.g. "by * * *" are not regarded as pseudonyms. Neither are initials,

---

[1] Can be seen at most public libraries. "Dictionary of Anonymous and Pseudonymous English Literature" (Samuel Halkett and John Laing). New and enlarged edition by Dr. James Kennedy, W. H. Smith and A. P. Johnson. Oliver and Boyd. 1926–34. 7v.

like "J. E.," "M.P.," "W. E. S. T.," since the cataloguer does not know whether a real name is represented or not, and, if a real name, whether the first or last or any other initial is the first letter of the surname. Also excluded from the pseudonymous class are indefinite phrases, such as "by a lover of children," "by an ex-soldier," "by one who looked on," and the common practice of a writer describing himself as author of another work. All such books are classed as anonymous and, unless the authors can be discovered, main entries are made under titles, not under devices, initials, or descriptions, although references can be given from these (Rule 19).

E.g. *Main entry*

                                                                 210

EGYPT.

    Egypt; or, The double land and its stone records. By W.E.S.T. Education Society's Press, Bycuilla, 1886.

Reference

    W.E.S.T.

        see

EGYPT.

Reference

    T., W.E.S.

        see

EGYPT.

84 CLASSIFICATION AND CATALOGUING

Sagas and many folk tales usually come into a group called by cataloguers the "anonymous classics." The authors are many and often unknown, while such works have appeared under a variety of titles, especially in translations. An excellent example is the Arabian nights. English title-pages may give, "The book of the thousand and one nights," "The thousand nights and a night," "The Arabian nights' entertainments," "Stories from the Arabian nights," "Tales from the thousand and one nights," "Aladdin and other tales from the Arabian nights," etc. First word title entry is impossible, since copies of the work would be scattered all over the catalogue, so a fixed title, e.g. Arabian nights, must be selected as the heading and all versions put under this. Added entries will be made for editors, translators, etc.

E.g. *Main entry*

    ARABIAN nights.   398.2

        Stories from the Arabian nights, retold by Laurence Housman. Hodder, 1931. Illus.

Added entry

    HOUSMAN, Laurence.   398.2
    ARABIAN nights.

        Stories from the Arabian nights, retold by Laurence Housman. Hodder, 1931. Illus.

A reference from the vernacular title may be required and in some cases entry under the vernacular is preferred, e.g. "Chanson de Roland" rather than "Song of Roland" (Rule 20).

The Bible and its parts come into this group. The heading will naturally be "Bible," though one enterprising cataloguing student tried putting it under "God"! Complete copies of the Bible are simple, but difficulties arise over selections, separate copies of the Old or New Testaments, and individual books. A scheme of subdivision should be adopted.

E.g.
    BIBLE.
    BIBLE. Selections.
    BIBLE. Old Testament.
    BIBLE. Old Testament. Selections.
    BIBLE. Old Testament. Genesis.
    BIBLE. Old Testament. Exodus.
                etc.
    BIBLE. New Testament.
    BIBLE. New Testament. Selections.
    BIBLE. New Testament. St. Matthew.
                etc.

Added entries should be made for editors, translators, etc., and there should be references from specific parts (Rule 21). For further details, the cataloguer is referred to the Anglo-American code, Rule 119.

Miscellaneous collections, generally made by one man from the work of many others, give rise to the problem of editor versus title main entry. As a rule, the editor is to be preferred. Anthologies like Palgrave's "Golden treasury" and Laurence Housman's "War letters of fallen Englishmen" are known and will be looked for under Palgrave or Housman. There can always be an added entry under title. But some collections are better known by title, and for these the procedure should be reversed (Rule 22).

Title entry is preferred for serial publications, like almanacs, year-books, and periodicals (Rule 23). Editors, if any, are not so well-known and change after some years. Year-books published by societies come under the rules for corporate authorship. (*See* previous chapter.)

Encyclopaedias and dictionaries have main entry under editor unless, as in the case of the "Encyclopædia Britannica," the work is better known by title (Rule 24).

Series entry is not important and may be omitted, but some librarians find it convenient when a series is well known, like "English men of letters." The full title of the series (excluding articles at the beginning) is taken as the heading. Underneath is given a list of books in that series which may be found in the library. The entries may be arranged according to volume number, by author, or by subject. It is usual to put several entries on one card, leaving gaps for missing volumes. Only volume number, author, title, and class mark need be given. Accession marks have to be recorded on the back of the card, as there will be several —one for each book (Rule 25).

If desired, a reference can be made from the name of the editor, or editors, to the title of the series, but this is not usually necessary.

E.g.

>   5
>   LOEB classical library; edited by T. E.
>   Page, etc.
>   v. 33 HORATIUS FLACCUS, Quintus.
>   Odes and epodes.   874
>   v. 34
>   v. 35 TACITUS, Caius Cornelius. Dia-
>   logues, Agricola, and Germania.   878

The series entry may take several cards. For each overflow one, the heading is repeated and the card numbered.

Rules for title entry

16. *Choice of heading.*—Title entry should generally be made under the first word of the title, exclusive of articles. In exceptional cases, some other word may be taken as heading.

17. *Added entries.*—Make an added entry for any striking title, provided it does not express the subject of the book.

18. *Anonymous.*—Enter an anonymous work under the author, if he can be traced, with added entry under title. Anonymous works of undiscovered authorship have main entry under title.

19. *Initials, etc.*—Initials, typographical devices, vague or lengthy descriptions, are not to be regarded as pseudonyms. Treat any book with such a substitute for the author's name as anonymous, according to Rule 18.

20. *Sagas, folk-tales, etc.*—Enter under the best-known English title, with a reference, when necessary, from the vernacular. Enter under the vernacular if better known. Make added entries under names of editors, translators, etc.

21. *Bible.*—Enter complete Bibles, or selections, under the word BIBLE, making a subheading for Selections. Separate copies of the Old Testament, or New Testament, are to be entered under BIBLE. Old Testament, or BIBLE. New Testament. A further subdivision is made for each book, e.g. BIBLE. Old Testament. Genesis. Make appropriate references from specific parts back to the general heading, and added entries under names of editors, translators, etc.

22. *Anthologies and miscellaneous collections.*—Collections of poems, plays, etc., taken from the works of several authors, are to be entered under the compiler or editor, unless better known by title, when title main entry is to be preferred. Make appropriate added entry.

23. *Serials.*—Serial publications, such as almanacs, yearbooks, periodicals, are to be entered under title. If, however, they are issued by cor-

porate bodies, they come under the rules for corporate authorship.

24. *Encyclopaedias, dictionaries.*—Encyclopaedias and dictionaries are to be entered under editor, unless better known by title when title main entry is preferred.

25. *Series.*—Make an added entry for an important series under the title of the series. Include in this entry a list of the works in the library belonging to the set.

CHAPTER SEVEN

SUBJECT AND FORM CATALOGUES

GENERAL PRINCIPLES

IN cataloguing, a subject heading may either be a word or phrase indicating the subject, e.g. Painting, School libraries, Thirty years' war; or, some symbol representing the subject, e.g. the Dewey Decimal class mark 750 instead of the word Painting. Whether the heading is a subject name or a class mark depends on the type of catalogue. There are three kinds of subject catalogues, the Alphabetical-subject, the Alphabetical-classed, and the Classified. The popular Dictionary catalogue consists of an Author and Title catalogue, mixed with an Alphabetical-subject, to form one file.

The first duty of a subject catalogue is to bring together books which treat of the same specific subject. In Mathematics, the Arithmetic books should be separated from those on Geometry. Here the Alphabetical-subject catalogue stops. The fundamental rule of this type of catalogue is specific, not class, entry. The technical definition is, "A catalogue arranged alphabetically by subject heads, usually without subdivisions. C. Davison's "The origin of earthquakes" would be entered directly under EARTH-

SUBJECT AND FORM CATALOGUES

QUAKES, and Rogers' "The gramophone handbook" under GRAMOPHONES.

If the catalogue is an Alphabetical-classed, then these specific subjects are arranged under broader groups or classes. That is to say, the Alphabetical-classed catalogue consists of classes, arranged in alphabetical order, and subdivided alphabetically into specific subjects. "The origin of earthquakes" would not be under EARTHQUAKES, but under its class GEOLOGY, which would have a subdivision for Earthquakes. "The gramophone handbook" would have as heading MUSIC-Gramophones.

The third kind of subject catalogue, the Classified, carries the process a step further, since classes and sub-divisions are arranged systematically, not according to the accidental positions of class or subject names in the alphabet. Such a catalogue follows whatever scheme of classification the library has adopted and uses the class marks as headings. Our earthquake book would have as subject heading 551, if Dewey (abridged) were used; P3 in Cheltenham; and DH in Bliss. To analyse the Dewey number, as an example, 500 is Science, 550 Geology, and 551 Physical and dynamic geology, including volcanoes and earthquakes.

Before discussing these catalogues in detail, some general points ought to be considered.

The cataloguer is particularly warned against assigning subject headings without looking any further than the title-page. Titles can be most deceptive, and often are incomplete descriptions. "The eagle's nest" by Ruskin deals with Art, not Eagles. "Way stations" by Elizabeth Robins has nothing to do with railway stations, but is a collection of speeches, lectures, etc., on the woman's movement. "The boy who found out" is the title of a life of Henri Fabre.

When a book is classified, one place has to be selected in the tables, since it cannot go in more than one place on the shelves (except in rare cases when a second copy is purchased). "The mind of the artist: thoughts and sayings of painters and sculptors . . ." is a contribution to two subjects, Painting and Sculpture. If placed at Art in general, it will be lost to both specific branches. A decision has to be made as to which subject is the more important, and the book classified accordingly. But in subject cataloguing, a card can be placed under each subject. Hebe Spaull's "The Baltic states: Latvia, Lithuania and Esthonia" can have an entry under each country. It is not practical to enter under too many subjects, and, usually, if a book deals with more than three, it is catalogued under an inclusive heading, but the individual cataloguer must decide whether detailed entries are advisable or not.

THE ALPHABETICAL-SUBJECT OR DICTIONARY CATALOGUE

The Dictionary catalogue consists of author, title, and subject entries arranged in one sequence, subject entry always being "added" (i.e. secondary), and the headings identical with those used in the Alphabetical-subject catalogue. Some libraries like the single file, particularly as books by and about an author come together. Others prefer an Author and Title catalogue, and separate Alphabetical-subject. As subject entry is the same in both cases, the two are discussed together, and it must be understood that everything said about this type of entry in the Dictionary applies equally well to the Alphabetical-subject. Although subject is the only type of entry in the latter, it is convenient to use the same "added entry" style, as this helps in sub-arranging by author books with the same subject headings.

E.g.

      FERNS.   587
     STEP, Edward.

        Wayside and woodland ferns. Warne, 1908. Illus. (Wayside and woodland series)

The basis of the Dictionary catalogue is the rule of specific entry. "The life of the bee," by Maeterlinck, has the heading BEES, not INSECTS. "A first book about Shakespeare" goes under SHAKESPEARE, William, not ENGLISH literature.

The definition states "arranged alphabetically by subject heads, usually without subdivision." Some subdivision is inevitable, but it is strictly limited to certain kinds. We may subdivide a subject according to forms. Thus, though separate branches of Science, like

Chemistry, Physics, etc., must be entered under their separate names not under the main class, yet we may subdivide Science into forms, like Essays, Encyclopaedias, History. In such cases, the books deal with Science, but the matter may be arranged in a special way, as in the literary form of an essay, or treated from a special viewpoint, e.g. historical. Secondly, the subject may be limited to a geographical region, e.g. "Bird life in Devon," which must be distinguished from works on the subject connected with other localities. Thirdly, period subdivision may be required. This is generally expressed by dates, e.g. ENGLAND—History—1485 to 1603.

Subdivision must be distinguished from compound subject headings, which are often inverted. These may range from two to several words.

E.g.
>ADULT education.
>CHURCH of England.
>ILLUMINATION of books and manuscripts.

Such compound names are not regarded as subdivisions of more general subjects, although there may be a rearrangement of the words to bring a heading close to other related ones. If the heading Economic geography is inverted and used in the form GEOGRAPHY, Economic, then it follows the general heading GEOGRAPHY in G, rather than being separated in the catalogue under E. Inversion depends on whether any advantage is to be

SUBJECT AND FORM CATALOGUES 95

gained through its use. In some cases, it would be absurd. No one would look for Nature study under STUDY, Nature.

Below are given examples of entry under a set of related subjects. It will be seen that the general one comes first, next general subdivided by form, region, etc., and then the more specific subjects that have compound names and are generally branches of the first. Entries and references must be filed in this order.

General

      ARCHITECTURE.   720
ALLEN, Phoebe.

    Peeps at architecture. Black, 1924. Illus.

General

      ARCHITECTURE.   720
LETHABY, W   R

    Architecture. Thornton Butterworth, 1929. Illus. (Home university library)

General divided by region, form, etc.

      ARCHITECTURE—England.   720
GODFREY, Walter H

    The story of architecture in England. Batsford, 1928-31. 2v. Illus.

General divided by region, form, etc.

> ARCHITECTURE—History.   720
> STATHAM, H   Heathcote.
>
> A short critical history of architecture. Batsford, 1927. Illus.

More specific subjects with inverted compound names

> ARCHITECTURE, Domestic.   728
> VIOLLET-LE-DUC, Eugène Emmanuel.
>
> How to build a house: an architectural novelette; translated by B. Bucknall. Low, 1874.

More specific subjects with inverted compound names

> ARCHITECTURE, Gothic.   723
> BROWNE, Edith A
>
> Gothic architecture. Second edition. Black, 1928. Illus.

Entry under the specific subject suits the reader who wants information on a small section of knowledge, but is not so convenient for the one studying a broader group. When Architecture is turned up, only general works on the subject will be found there. More specific branches, whose name consists of another word and architecture, will be found after the general, but others will be scattered all over the catalogue. To show what specific headings have been used and so prevent the reader from missing any, or wasting time by looking up ones not in the catalogue, the "see also" reference has been devised. Popularly expressed, this carries the message, "For further information, look elsewhere!" It guides the reader from general to specific and also to cognate, related subjects. For example, Architecture needs a "see also" to its cognate BUILDING. This reference card comes after works on the subject, but before form and regional, etc., subdivisions. Between W. R. Lethaby's "Architecture" and Walter H. Godfrey's "The story of architecture in England," is the "see also" reference card.

E.g.
>
> ARCHITECTURE
> *see also*
> BUILDING
> CATHEDRALS
> CHURCHES
> THEATRES

If the library acquires a book on the architecture of temples, this will be added to the card. Do not make "see also" references to specific headings which have not been used, i.e. under which there will be no catalogue entries.

When it has been decided to invert a heading, e.g. ARCHITECTURE, Gothic, then some guidance is needed for the reader who looks up GOTHIC architecture, or he may assume the library has nothing on the subject. The message of the "see also" reference was, "for further information, look elsewhere!" The "see" reference means, "Nothing here! Look elsewhere!" In author cataloguing, "see" references were employed to direct readers from rejected headings to ones which had been used, such as reference from the second part of a compound surname to the first. They have the same function in subject cataloguing.

E.g.
      ENGLAND, Church of
         see
      CHURCH of England.

      SEISMOLOGY
         see
      EARTHQUAKES.

Consistency in the selection of subject headings is very important. Otherwise, material on the same subject may be scattered under a variety of headings. Books on Primitive man could be entered under MAN, Prehistoric; MAN, Primitive; PREHISTORIC man; PRIMITIVE man; or even, EARLY man. Unless the cataloguer works to a list of subject headings and records all decisions, he can easily put books on the same subject in different places. References, too, can get completely out of control, unless some system of noting them is adopted. The cataloguer can compile his own list, but it saves a great deal of work to use one of the standard ones, writing in any modifications. The most satisfactory of these for school library purposes, is Sears' "List of

SUBJECT AND FORM CATALOGUES 99

subject headings for small libraries." It is published by the H. W. Wilson Company of New York, and costs approximately fifteen shillings.

The third edition of Sears (1933) has a very useful introduction on pages xi to xviii, giving directions to the beginner in subject work. It explains the system of marking headings with ticks, to show these have been adopted in the catalogue, when to make "see" and "see also" references, and how to add headings for new subjects. The author sums up the processes involved when assigning a subject heading for the first time to any book. ". . . The steps are: (1) to check the subject itself, (2) to make and check any "see" references to the subject that are necessary, i.e. from synonyms or forms which are not to be used, (3) to make and check any "see also" references from related subjects to this new subject . . . (4) to make and check any "see also" references necessary from this new subject to other aspects of the subjects. . . ."

Supposing one has a book on the collecting of postage stamps. Shall it go under POSTAGE stamps, or STAMPS, Postage; or STAMP collecting? Sears' gives the heading POSTAGE stamps. Underneath are suggested "see" references from PHILATELY and STAMPS, Postage, and a "see also" from COLLECTORS and collecting. If there are other books in the library catalogued under this subject heading, then the heading and references will have been ticked in the printed list, so only one card—the actual entry for the new book—need be written. Otherwise, reference cards are made out and then the headings ticked, so that they need not be done next time. There may already be a card for the "see also" reference, but not containing the present heading. If the library has one or more works on Book collecting, then there would be a "see also" from COLLECTORS and collecting. Now there is a book on Stamp collecting, the heading selected for that subject is added to the card.

E.g. *Entry card*

    POSTAGE stamps.   383
    PHILLIPS, Stanley.
        The beginner's book of stamp collecting. Sampson Low, 1934. Illus.

"*See*" *ref.*

    STAMPS, Postage
       see
  POSTAGE stamps.

"*See*" *ref.*

    PHILATELY
      see
  POSTAGE stamps.

"*See also*" *ref.*

    COLLECTORS and collecting
      see also
  BOOK collecting
  POSTAGE stamps

Collecting cigarette cards is becoming a recognized hobby. In the 1933 edition of Sears there is no provision for it, so if a library acquires a book on the subject, a suitable heading would have to be inserted in the printed list, e.g. CIGARETTE cards. This heading would need a "see" reference from CARDS, Cigarette, and would have to be added to the subjects following the "see also" of COLLECTORS and collecting.

When making new headings, two rules should be observed. First, prefer plural to singular terms, e.g. ELEPHANTS rather than ELEPHANT. The plural is inclusive and does away with any necessity for a definite article and its awkward inversion, e.g. ELEPHANT, The. Secondly, avoid the use of the ethnic adjective, except in cases of racial rather than geographical distinction, like literatures and languages. Thus we have ROME—History, but LATIN literature. Use England with History as a subdivision, not English history, but the phrase headings, ENGLISH language and ENGLISH literature.

Whether entry should be made under subject or country (and, in certain cases, ethnic adjective and subject), has been much debated. General opinion is that scientific and technical subjects should be entered under their subjects, with local subdivision, if necessary. The ornithologist, going to Sweden for a holiday, goes to BIRDS, not SWEDEN, if he is looking for a work on the Bird life of that country. The mining engineer expects to find all books on Mining together. It may be argued that the history specialist has the same claim to find everything under HISTORY, but if this is done there will be so many entries here that it will be confusing. Then it is very convenient to have subjects like History, Travel, Social life, Government, relating to specific countries under the countries. Hence the practice of only entering general works on History, under this heading, while histories of England go under ENGLAND —History.[1] The "see also" reference from History need not record the names of all the countries. One example makes the direction clear.

E.g.
>   HISTORY
>   see also subdivisions Antiquities, Foreign relations, History, Politics and government under names of countries, states, etc., e.g.
>   ENGLAND—History.

Beginners must guard against overloading the catalogue with unnecessary entries. Above all, avoid entering a book under both general and specific headings. For example, a book on Skating can only be entered under SKATING, not under WINTER sports as well. The "see also" reference directs the reading from general to specific heading, and this is sufficient.

[1] Sears prefers the heading GREAT Britain to ENGLAND. This is better in a library that stocks government publications where author entry must be GREAT Britain, but school libraries have very few of these and will probably prefer the heading ENGLAND.

CHAPTER EIGHT

SUBJECT AND FORM CATALOGUES (*continued*)

THE ALPHABETICAL-SUBJECT OR DICTIONARY CATALOGUE (*continued*)

THE Dictionary (or Alphabetical-subject) is undoubtedly the easiest kind of subject catalogue for general use. Hence its wide popularity. The reader who wants information on a specific subject like Pirates, goes straight to PIRATES, instead of being obliged to hunt through all the cards on VOYAGES and travels. If he should turn to VOYAGES and travels first, a "see also" reference will direct him to PIRATES.

Opponents of this type of subject catalogue complain that too much time is wasted in following up references and consulting different headings. They argue that a reader going for a holiday to Scotland may want to see books on Edinburgh, Glasgow, etc., as well as general works on the country. He may be interested in the flora or fauna and have to look under a variety of other headings, such as BIRDS—Scotland, BOTANY—Scotland. Then, there is always the possibility that some vital heading has been missed.

Such a subject catalogue must be well done. That is, headings and references must be assigned consistently —preferably from a printed list like Sears. It is no use

104 CLASSIFICATION AND CATALOGUING

attempting to compile such a catalogue without "see" and "see also" references, as they are fundamental. Great care must be taken, too, not to make references to headings under which no books have been entered. Slackness on the part of the cataloguer has more disastrous results in this type of catalogue than in any other.

The scattering of specific subjects according to the position of their names in the alphabet is illogical, but convenient for easy reference. Besides, it is impossible to achieve complete proximity of related subjects, even in a classification scheme. There are too many aspects. A subject like Colour may come under Chemistry, Aesthetics, Optics, and Painting in a classification, that is, under 540, 701, 535, 750 in Dewey. The Dictionary catalogue would enter all books on Colour under the subject name COLOUR, thus collocating them, no matter whether they dealt with the chemical, aesthetic, optical or artistic aspect. "See also" references would guide the reader from Chemistry, etc. Subject entry in the Dictionary catalogue is so different from subject classification that the two make a useful combination. There are advantages in having one method of subject arrangement for books on the shelves and another for entries in the catalogue.

Many librarians prefer to have one complete catalogue, instead of two or three, and the single file of author, title, and subject entries in the Dictionary adds to the popularity of this catalogue. Works by

Shakespeare are followed by works about Shakespeare. There is the alternative method of keeping subject entries apart and forming them into a separate Alphabetical-subject catalogue, but at any time this and the Author and Title can be changed into a Dictionary.

If the two are separated, then it is advisable to treat them in the same way as the Dictionary, when cataloguing. Make the author card the main entry and record tracings (i.e. list of other entries and references, see Chapter Five) on the back, while the subject card or cards should be set out in the usual added entry style. The importance of tracings in any kind of catalogue cannot be over-emphasized, but to attempt the Dictionary without such a record is suicidal. Worn-out books have to be withdrawn and it is often necessary to make minor alterations to cards for books in stock. A cataloguer can easily forget what added entries and references have been made (particularly subject ones), with the result that a book may be withdrawn, but some cards for it left in the catalogue. Alterations are made to three or four cards for a particular book, and the fifth overlooked. Nothing is more useless than an inaccurate catalogue, and this is what a Dictionary one will certainly become in a number of years if tracings are omitted.

THE ALPHABETICAL-CLASSED CATALOGUE

The Alphabetical-classed catalogue may be defined as a subject catalogue in which knowledge is divided into a number of broad classes, these being arranged in alphabetical order. Each class is subdivided into numerous broad alphabetical divisions. Entry is under the class and division, while "see" references guide the reader from more specific subject headings to the general ones in use, the reverse of the Alphabetical-subject or Dictionary where reference is from general to specific, and occasionally to cognate subjects.

To compile an Alphabetical-classed catalogue, the librarian must decide on the classes. The school curriculum may influence his choice, or he may copy those belonging to a classification scheme. For purposes of illustration here, the main classes of the Cheltenham scheme have been used as a foundation for constructing such a catalogue. In the scheme, each class is designated by a capital letter and their order is as follows:

- A Theology
- B Philosophy
- C Sociology
- D History
- E Language and Literature (General). English
- F French Language and Literature
- G German Language and Literature
- H Italian and other Romance Languages and Literatures
- J Spanish and Portuguese Languages and Literatures
- K Classics (Greek and Latin)
- L Eastern European, Oriental and other Languages, etc.

SUBJECT AND FORM CATALOGUES 107

M Science
P Geology and Geography.
R Applied Science. Technology
S Fine Arts
W Junior Library
Y Fiction Library
Z Generalia

These classes must be rearranged in alphabetical order, the class marks (i.e. letters) being dropped. Certain classes, W and Y, will not be needed, and E to L could be kept together under the heading LANGUAGES and literatures. Useful arts is a term that will cover both Applied science and Technology. If the phrases Useful arts and Fine arts are inverted, they will come next to each other in the catalogue. We thus get ten main groups or classes.

> ARTS, Fine
> ARTS, Useful
> GENERALIA
> GEOGRAPHY and geology
> HISTORY
> LANGUAGES and literatures
> PHILOSOPHY
> SCIENCE
> SOCIOLOGY
> THEOLOGY

Each group is subdivided and the subdivisions arranged alphabetically under the classes. LANGUAGES and literatures is broken up into English, French,

German, etc. In the Cheltenham scheme, the nine divisions of Class M (Science) are as follows:—

>   General
>   Astronomy
>   Mathematics
>   Physics
>   Chemistry
>   Biology
>   Botany
>   Zoology
>   Man

In the Alphabetical-classed catalogue, these groups must be rearranged alphabetically. "General" is not required, as general works on Science are entered under the class heading without subdivision. So under Science we get:

>   SCIENCE
>   SCIENCE—Astronomy
>   SCIENCE—Biology
>   SCIENCE—Botany
>   SCIENCE—Chemistry
>   SCIENCE—Man
>   SCIENCE—Mathematics
>   SCIENCE—Physics
>   SCIENCE—Zoology

Subdivision can be carried further, but is hardly practical as such long headings are involved, e.g. SCIENCE—Zoology—Birds. Entries are sub-arranged by author under the classes, as shown below.

SUBJECT AND FORM CATALOGUES 109

Extract from part of an A.C. catalogue

    SCIENCE—Physics.   537
SOUTHERNS, Leonard.

    Electricity and the structure of matter. Oxford University Press, 1925. Illus. (World's manuals)

    SCIENCE—Physics.   530
THOMPSON, *Sir* J   Arthur.

    What the world is made of. Newnes, 1929. Illus. (Outline library)

    SCIENCE—Zoology.   591.5
ANNIXTER, Paul.

    Wilderness ways. Harrap, 1931. Illus.

    SCIENCE—Zoology.   595.7
BALFOUR-BROWNE, F

    Concerning the habits of insects. Cambridge University Press, 1925. Illus.

    SCIENCE—Zoology.   598.1
BERRIDGE, W   S

    Marvels of reptile life. Thornton Butterworth, 1926. Illus.

SCIENCE—Zoology. 597
BOULENGER, E   G

    Queer fish and other inhabitants of the rivers and oceans. Partridge, 1925. Illus.

SCIENCE—Zoology. 598
CHAFFE, Allen.

    Penn the penguin. Murray, 1934. Illus.

SCIENCE—Zoology. 595.7
CHEESMAN, Evelyn.

    Everyday doings of insects. Harrap, 1930. Illus.

Author and title entries are usually kept separate and not mixed with subject entries of the Alphabetical-classed, but there is nothing to prevent this being done, if wished.

Besides the subject entries, "see" reference cards, directing readers from specific to more general headings, are needed. These are filed in their appropriate alphabetical places.

E.g.
    INSECTS
      see
SCIENCE—Zoology.

SUBJECT AND FORM CATALOGUES

    PENGUINS
      see
    SCIENCE—Zoology.

    ZOOLOGY
      see
    SCIENCE—Zoology.

It will be seen that the Alphabetical-classed catalogue can only provide for very broad subject division, and under each heading comes a long array of cards, sub-arranged in alphabetical order of authors. The reader studying Birds has to hunt through all the cards of SCIENCE—Zoology to collect his material. For someone who wants information on a particular kind of bird, e.g. Penguins, the position is even worse. On the other hand, to break up the groups into further subdivision means such impossibly long headings,

E.g.
    SCIENCE—Zoology—Birds—Penguins.

    LITERATURE—English—Sixteenth century
      —Shakespeare.

The arrangement is as illogical as that of the Dictionary catalogue, while the gathering together of subjects in broad groups alphabetically emphasizes the artificiality. In the Cheltenham classification, the groups under Science are arranged so that cognates like Mathematics, Physics, Chemistry come together. In the Alphabetical-classed catalogue their positions in the alphabet determine their places. Yet, any other arrangement is impossible, since there is no notation and the catalogue is fundamentally an alphabetical one.

The Alphabetical-classed catalogue is a hybrid form and has the faults of Dictionary and Classified, without their virtues. It is very little used in libraries, so there are no printed guides to its compilation or aids to choice of headings, while pupils are unlikely to encounter this type of subject catalogue in other libraries.

THE CLASSIFIED CATALOGUE

In the Classified catalogue, names of subjects are not used as headings, but the classification symbols assigned to those subjects in a book scheme, e.g. Dewey, Cheltenham, Bliss. The scheme chosen should be the one used in the arrangement of books on the shelves. In a Dictionary catalogue, a book about Shakespeare would be entered directly under his name, e.g. SHAKESPEARE, William. The Alphabetical-classed would have some such heading as LITERATURE—English; or, this could be further divided, e.g. Sixteenth century—Shakespeare. But, in the Classified, the class mark would be used, e.g. 822.3 (Dewey), E15.6 (Cheltenham), YF (Bliss). In any other but the Classified catalogue the class mark is usually placed in the top right-hand corner, although some librarians prefer it to follow the entry. So long as one position is adopted and rigidly adhered to, the exact place does not matter in the

SUBJECT AND FORM CATALOGUES

catalogues which have been discussed so far, but in the Classified it must either be above the author's name, or in front of it. Filing is strictly according to class order, with sub-arrangement by author.

E.g.

    622
    WILLIAMS, Archibald.

        The romance of modern mining. Seeley, 1923. Illus. (Library of romance)

or, more usual style

  622 WILLIAMS, Archibald.

        The romance of modern mining. Seeley, 1923. Illus. (Library of romance)

If a book can be classified in more than one place, a choice has to be made for the classification of the book itself, but entries can be duplicated in the catalogue under alternative numbers. Such "added" entries, must also contain the class mark where the book is shelved. It is usually placed below the entry and preceded by the words, *Shelved at*.

E.g. *Main entry*

  750 DICK, Stewart.

        Hours in the National Gallery. Duckworth, 1925. Illus.

Added entry

  914 DICK, Stewart.
   21

      Hours in the National Gallery. Duckworth, 1925. Illus.

Shelved at 750

The Classified catalogue must stand alone, since its entries cannot be successfully mixed with alphabetical name headings. A library has to keep a separate Author and Title catalogue. Thus, entry under the shelving mark in the Classified catalogue will be the main entry, and this should contain tracings of class numbers of any added cards. For example, on the back of the above main entry, will be noted, *Added entry* 914.21.

In addition, the Classified catalogue needs an alphabetical index of subjects, with their corresponding class marks. No book titles will be mentioned in this index. It is merely an index to the scheme, like the printed ones with which most classification systems are equipped. It is possible to use a printed index, but more satisfactory to make one's own on cards. Many of the subjects listed in the index to a scheme like Dewey, will not be represented by books in the average school library. In other cases, extra entries may be required. Index entries are very brief and consist only of names of subjects and class marks,

E.g.

    PAINTING   750

The Classified catalogue is by far the simplest and easiest type to compile. It is systematic, arranging subjects in groups. The notation keeps these groups and subdivisions in a rational order, not artificial like an alphabetical one. Although in groups, specific subjects are kept together, since subdivision is not limited through fear of long headings, as in the Alphabetical-classed. Headings are brief, easily arranged, and soon comprehended by pupils who use a classified library. Furthermore, the Subject index assists readers who want material on a subject, but do not know the class mark. If a boy turns up Reptiles, for example, he finds an entry REPTILES 598.1. Then, he can either go straight to the shelves and examine the books marked 598.1, or he can turn to that heading in the Classified catalogue. The catalogue is more comprehensive, as books may be out on loan, but entry cards remain. Also, there might be a book on Insects, Birds and Reptiles, which would be classified on the shelves at 590, but have extra catalogue cards under 595.7, 598 and 598.1.

Another advantage of the Classified catalogue is that it does away with the need for a Shelf list. As the catalogue follows the order of books on the shelves, this can be used for stock-taking purposes. Added entries will have to be ignored and any books on special oversize or reference shelves dealt with separately, but otherwise there is no difficulty in using the catalogue as a Shelf list.

CLASSIFICATION AND CATALOGUING

Extract from part of a Classified catalogue

796 SHARP, Arthur.

    The rucksack way. Jenkins, 1934.

797 HEDGES, S   G

    The swim book. Methuen, 1934. Illus.

797 HOBBS, Edward W

    Model sailing boats: their design, building, and sailing. Cassell, 1923.

797 VENNER, R   C

    Swimming for all. Bell, 1931. Illus.

798 FAWCETT, William.

    Elements of horsemanship. Field, 1932. Illus.

799 CLAXTON, William J

    The boy's book of angling and rambling by river, pond, and sea. Epworth Press, 1910. Illus.

799 NEWBOLT, *Sir* Henry.

    The book of good hunting. Longmans, 1925. Illus.

FORM ENTRY

Certain types of books do not have subject entry. Such entry may be impossible because the book deals with

SUBJECT AND FORM CATALOGUES

so many subjects, e.g. a general encyclopaedia; or, it would never be looked for under subject, e.g. no one would turn to FALL of man, or GARDEN of Eden, expecting to find under either of these headings a catalogue entry for Milton's "Paradise lost."

In such cases the "form" of the book is more important than its subject. "Form" is commonly concerned with the arrangement and presentation of the subject matter. There is the alphabetical (or, occasionally classified) arrangement of an encyclopaedia or dictionary, the metrical pattern of a poem, etc. A book like Courthope's "History of English poetry" has a subject entry under ENGLISH poetry, but Palgrave's "Golden treasury" would be entered under ENGLISH poetry as a form heading.

Form entries are made in subject catalogues for encyclopaedias and other reference works, as well as for anthologies and collections. Generally, they are omitted for individual literary texts, since these are known by author and can be found under author headings, so there is no need to repeat the entries again under ENGLISH poetry, ENGLISH drama, etc.; or, LITERATURE—English; or, 821, 822, etc. It all depends on the library. If it is felt that form entries in these cases are useful, then they should certainly be made.

INDEX

Accessions number 56, 86
Added entry 72–75, 79, 80–81, 82, 93, 113, 115
Alphabetical-classed catalogue 50, 90–91, 105–112
Alphabetical-subject catalogue 50, 90, 92–105
Alternatives in classification schemes 28, 35
Anglo-American code 61
Anonymous books 81–85
Archbishops as authors 69–70
Arrangement in catalogues 52, 95–96, 109–110, 113, 116
Author entry 59–78
Author and Title catalogues 50, 59–89
Authorship, Corporate 59, 75–76, 78
Authorship, Individual 59–75, 76–78

Bible 85
Bishops as authors 69–70
Bliss classification 15, 31–36
Broad classification 17
Brown's Subject classification 15

Capitals 54
Card catalogue 51–52

Catalogue—Purpose 49
Catalogues—Display 51–52
Catalogues—Kinds 49–50
Change of name in authors 61, 64–65
Cheltenham classification 15, 26–31, 106–107, 111
Class mark 12, 56
Classical authors 70
Classification schemes—
  Bliss 15, 31–36
  Brown's subject 15
  Cheltenham 15, 26–31, 106–107, 111
  Dewey 15, 20–26
  "Home-made" 15
  Library of Congress 15, 17
Classified catalogue 50, 91, 112–116
Classifying books 41–48
Close classification 11, 17, 45
Collation 55–56
Corporate authorship 59, 75–76, 78

Dewey-Decimal classification 15, 20–26
Dictionary catalogue 50, 90, 92–105

Edition 54

Entry, Added 72–75, 79, 80–81, 82, 93, 113, 115
Entry, Main 72, 73, 114
Entry, Make-up of 52–56

Fixed location 13
Forenames, Entry under 70
Form in cataloguing 93–94, 117
Form in classification 42

Guide cards 52

Hyphenated surnames 62–63

Imprint 55
Index to classification schemes 13, 18, 44, 46
Index to classified catalogue 114–115
Initials 60, 83

Library of Congress classification 15, 17
Literal mnemonics 25, 34
Location, Fixed 12
Location mark 56
Logical order 17, 25, 31–33

Main entry 72, 73, 114
Marking books 39–40
Married women as authors 64–65
Mnemonics, Literal 29, 34
Modifications in classification schemes 18–19, 23, 37

Name catalogue 50
Noblemen as authors 61, 68–69
Notation 11, 17–18, 24, 28, 32, 33–35

Oversize books 46, 56, 115

Parallel classification 47
Prefixes to surnames 63–64
Pseudonyms 61, 70–72, 82
Punctuation 54–55

References—
  "See" 62–63, 72, 98, 99, 106, 110
  "See also" 97, 99, 102, 104

Series 46, 56, 86–87
Sheaf catalogue 51
Shelf guiding 40
Shelf list 38, 39, 115
Specific entry 93, 96, 104
Subject catalogues 50, 90–116
Subject heading lists 98–101
Surnames, Hyphenated 62–63
Surnames with prefixes 63–64

Title entry 79–89
Title, Transcription of 53–55
Titles of address 65–70
Tracings 73–74, 105